NO BUNK JUST BS (BUSINESS SENSE)

50 Timely and Timeless Truths Business School Cannot Teach You!

Sheila Newman Glazov

Book Title

The title of the book came from one of my father's preferred expressions that was a 1940's slang term. My father rarely used profanity. However, he would say, "That's a bunch of bunk." referring to something that he thought was absurd, ridiculous, nonsense, or untrue.

Peridot Productions

Library of Congress Catalog Card Number: 2018952202

1. Business   2. Memoir   3. Family   4. Nonfiction
5. Manufacturing

Praise for No Bunk, Just BS (Business Sense)

As a business leader, often pressed for time, I love the easy to read "memoir snippets." There's a uniquely authentic quality to the business sense shared as real correspondence between employer and employees. I expect every reader will find an anecdote that speaks to them.
TJ Butler, Chief Software Architect at Mesh Systems LLC

No Bunk, Just BS (Business Sense) should be required reading for anyone who wants valued, time-tested guidance about how to grow and prosper in their career (and life). Don't miss the opportunity to learn from a pro!
John Bond, Publishing Consultant/Riverwinds Consulting, Author of You Can Write and Publish, Second Edition

I love the timeless treasures in this book. Sheila, like her father, has a knack for delivering No Nonsense business tips that are as relevant today as they were decades ago. Employees that know they are appreciated are the keystone to success. I will definitely have my staff read this book so we can discuss how we, as a team, can further fine tune our customer's experience.
Jill Winalis Looff, Owner and Vice President, Signs By Tomorrow

I could not put it down. It's filled with inspirational life lessons. The stories are a quick read. I could relate to Mr. Newman because I had a personal insight into his personality and how he thought. I felt as if I knew him and would enjoying talking to him because I knew how he felt about his employees and how they felt about him.
Jeff Lewis, Owner, The Webs We Weave

No Bunk grabbed my attention from the get-go. Once I began reading, I couldn't put it down! Sheila Glazov delivers precious business gems in a direct, authentic, and meaningful way that are as relevant today as when they were initially penned.
Laurie Buchanan, PhD, holistic health practitioner, transformation life coach, author of Note to Self and The Business of Being

Sheila is an amazing author and an inspiration to all. Her latest book would be a beneficial read for my business partners and my employees. It would also be a great gift to give my clients.
Jad N. Lahoud, President & CEO, L&H Partners, Construction and Realty

As a business owner who was raised in retail, I find the information and wisdom in *No Bunk* extremely valuable. Business owners will take away nuggets that are immediately applicable to their company. In a world filled with "instant information" this book is a real keeper.
Caryn Amster, Author, <u>The Pied Piper of South Shore, Toys and Tragedy in Chicago</u>

Within every piece she authors, Sheila communicates clarity of purpose and a constancy of focus upon the true values that motivate and empower all of us. I look forward to gifting copies of this next book to all my associates and embracing it as a key tool in renewing how we do business.
Nedd Neddersen, President, IDM Hospitality Management

Sheila's work provides busy executives with wisdom and anecdotes that address how to maintain a sense of workplace community as technology and cultural shifts teeter us toward disengagement. Her approach is a refreshing primer on truths worth revisiting.
Marsha L. Turner, CAE, CEO, International Association of Lighting Designers (IALD)

Sheila is a thoughtful author who stimulates innovation around how leaders think. Any of her publications would be well worth the read and consideration for distribution within a leadership team.
Matthew Primack, PT, DPT, MBA, President, Advocate Christ Medical Center

Dedication

This book is a tribute to my beloved parents,
Alexander I. Newman and Sylvia F. Newman,
and their life and business partnership.

1953

NEW HOME OF
LAB-LINE INSTRUMENTS Inc.
Research & Laboratory Equipment

CONTINENTAL
CONSTRUCTION CO.

W. FRED DOLKE
ARCHITECT·ENGINEER

1963

1960

This book is dedicated to Julia M. Amorella,
my father's executive secretary,
for her devotedness and friendship.

No Bunk, Just BS

Table of Contents

No Bunk, Just BS

Message from the Author

Anticipatory Set

As an author and educator, I wanted to include an **Anticipatory Set,** which is an educational term to activate and engage your attention and prepare you in advance for your reading adventure and what to expect about my book.

My first concept of the book was a business memoir about Lab-Line Instruments, Inc., which was the laboratory equipment business my parents founded in 1952. I had planned on using my archive of Lab-Line *HI-LITER* newsletter articles that were filled with copious business and life lessons, inspiring stories and visionary wisdom, and enduring quotes as a vehicle to impart business advice.

However, like my other books, *NO BUNK, JUST BS (Business Sense)* took on a life of its own. The framework of this book evolved into two distinct sections: No Bunk Truths and Memoir. Each section is designed to educate and inspire:
1. People who have not had the opportunity to be taught fundamental business concepts and rapport building skills.
2. Experienced individuals who desire a refresher for their business and relationship capabilities.

Gender Clarification

NO BUNK, JUST BS (Business Sense) includes an anthology of articles that have been taken from Lab-Line *HI-LITER* Newsletters or memos. Whenever possible, I have given credit to the authors of an article or story.

Many of the stories, articles, or poems included male references (men, man, or his). They were written during a time when women seldom participated in society as decision makers and leaders in the business community, as they do now. Where it was appropriate, I took a little literary license to add female references (women, woman, or her). I know my mother and my father would highly approve of my revisions. They were respectful, grateful, and proud of the remarkable women and men who helped them build Lab-Line and achieve and maintain success that everyone enjoyed!

Book Cover
The colors on the *NO BUNK, JUST BS (Business Sense)* book cover represent two early Lab-Line catalog covers. The blue comes from the first catalog cover that was printed in 1952. The black and orange come from a catalog that was printed in 1964.

Book Plate
I have included a bookplate in the book to document your ownership of *NO BUNK, JUST BS (Business Sense)*. My father taught me, by his example, to sign all my books as he did with his strong signature of "Alexander I. Newman." The shape represents the original Lab-Line logo.

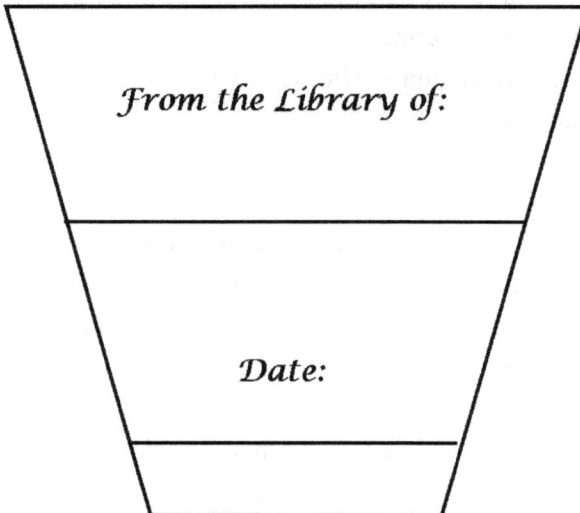

From the Library of:

Date:

Foreword

No Bunk, Just BS (Business Sense) 50 Timeless Truths Business School Cannot Teach You! is an ode to the power of business, family, and community.

I am the President and CEO of a retail business with roots dating back almost 60 years. In 1959, my grandfather founded the business; then my father successfully ran the family business for more than 30 years, before I joined full-time in 1998.

Like many other large and small companies, we spend a tremendous amount of time, effort, and energy, internally as well as through experienced consultants, developing programs aimed towards improving business performance, profitability and the workplace experience. Reading *No Bunk* reminded me that many times, the best and most enduring ideas are those that are common sense and easy to understand.

Sheila beautifully and creatively captures 50 of these *Truths* in her book. These truths are as relevant today as they were when the Newmans were building their business over 50 years ago and will be relevant for the next generation of business leaders, as they build for the future. Faithfully followed, these *Truths* will make any business endeavor more successful.

The more subtle, but just as important, realization for me from reading *No Bunk* is the important role business plays in our communities. At one level, businesses are important because of the very business in which they engage. However, at a deeper level, businesses are important because they provide a platform to make a difference in the lives of their employees, vendors, and customers.

The question for us as business leaders, managers, and enthusiasts is whether we will use that platform and embrace the responsibility that comes with it to make a positive difference in the lives of the people with whom we touch, as Alexander and Sylvia Newman did at the helm of Lab-Line Instruments.

We all need to answer this question, whether we are in a small or large business, family-run, or public. For me, *No Bunk* serves as a wake-up call and direct challenge to which I respond with an emphatic "YES." My response, however, will not just be something I say, but more importantly, actions that will be obvious to all those with whom our company touches. How will you answer that question?

In closing and on a very personal note, *No Bunk* is a beautiful and touching tribute by Sheila to her parents. I never had the honor to meet them, but I am sure they would be very proud of Sheila, though not surprised at all by her love and thoughtfulness.

Not only is *No Bunk, Just BS (Business Sense)* a testament to Sheila's respect for the work of her parents, but it also reflects the deep appreciation the many Lab-Line employees, vendors, and customers had for the business that made such a positive difference in their lives. These great gifts are the result of a lifetime of honorable work and timeless *Truths* to which we should all aspire.

Raymond J. Kayal, Jr.
President & CEO of Newslink Management Group, LLC

Introduction

No Bunk, Just BS (Business Sense) is not a Band-Aid® for your business problems. It's a blueprint to achieve and maintain business success; it features 50 timely and timeless truths business school cannot teach you!

No Bunk, Just BS delivers straight talk, logical suggestions, and candid solutions for business owners, leaders, managers, and team members.

No Bunk, Just BS is easy to read, educational, and encouraging. It provides readers with insightful and mindful solutions that de-bunk impersonal and cynical attitudes and trendy jargon. It teaches and restores uncomplicated business sense, satisfaction, and success in the workplace.

No Bunk, Just BS offers readers authentic and time-tested business knowledge and proficiencies that cannot be learned in business school. This anthology comprises 5 chapters. Each chapter includes 10 sensible anecdotes and adages, mindful acknowledgements and advice, and motivating stories and quotes that are prophetic and perpetual from the Lab-Line *HI-LITER* newsletters.

The ***No Bunk, Just BS*** chapters follow a logical sequence that helps readers develop, attain, and preserve their business success. The chapters include life-long lessons and fundamental business concepts for people who have not had the opportunity to be taught applicable business know-how and skills. For seasoned individuals who desire a refresher for their business knowledge there are constructive and practical tips to:

- Grow your business
- Promote exemplary and respectful leadership

- Value and encourage exceptional employees and teamwork
- Provide extraordinary customer service and client care
- Offer excellent products and services
- Achieve and maintain success

Changes in the global economy, technology, and social media admirably compel businesses to be more aware, inclusive, and accepting of minority, racial, cultural, gender, and religious differences. However, people in many businesses have often allowed means of inclusion and acceptance to diminish their candor, civility, compassion, customer service, client care, and commitment to employees, team members, and customers.

It's critical for a business community to re-examine how they conduct themselves. Businesses and individuals injured by economic and ethical wounds yearn for repair and healing. Learning from enduring and fundamental truths about building healthy and respectful relationships with others offers that healing and repair.

People seek genuine business leaders and managers who sincerely listen and respond to their basic need for appreciation of their attributes, abilities, and perspectives. *No Bunk, Just BS* provides practical and productive solutions to help and encourage people who crave humanity and authenticity in the workplace. *No Bunk, Just BS* offers readers that knowledge to achieve those goals!

The *No Bunk, Just BS* "retro" rhetoric and lessons for building a strong sense of community are unmistakable statements. The ethics and practices that were relevant to establish competitive and successful businesses in the mid-20th century are still valid today.

Fashion, home décor, hair styles, and cuisine dictate fads that temporarily capture attention, but ultimately fade out of style. *No Bunk, Just BS* teaches valued and valuable truths that *never* go out of style.

No Bunk, Just BS

NO BUNK JUST BS

(BUSINESS SENSE)

NO BUNK TRUTHS

No Bunk Truths Backstory: Lab-Line Newsletters

The genesis for *No Bunk, Just BS (Business Sense) 50 Timely and Timeless Truths Business School Cannot Teach You!* has been a long list of serendipitous events. As ideas for a family business memoir continued to wave at me, I recognized the priceless gift I had been given from my father and my mother.

The events began in April 2005, when I received a phone call from Bill Stutz, the Plant Supervisor, at Lab-Line Instruments. Lab-Line was a company that designed and sold laboratory equipment for scientific and medical research that my father and mother (both of blessed memory) founded in 1952. I was both surprised to hear Bill's voice and shocked when Bill explained that the building my father had designed and built in 1963 to house Lab-Line's expansion (the third home of the 53-year-old company) was going to be torn down.

Bill told me that Lab-Line had been purchased by a company that was moving its operations to Asia and was selling the 110,000 square foot building to another company that planned to tear it down and use the land for a parking lot. Then, Bill asked me if I would be interested going through the Lab-Line library, which still contained my father's books.

Urgency and sadness clenched my heart as I listened to the dreadful news. But I was delighted by Bill's thoughtfulness and generosity. I told Bill that my husband and I would drive to Lab-Line to save my father's library. A few days after Bill's call, my husband Jordan and I embarked on a remarkable journey to retrieve expected and unexpected treasures at Lab-Line.

Arriving at Lab-Line, we backed our truck into the loading dock and walked into the shipping and warehouse area. Muted emptiness greeted us.

The plant was filled with silent machinery, tagged for auction. It was void of Lab-Line's industrious employees and their congenial voices, who made it alive while they were designing, manufacturing, and shipping Lab-Line's laboratory apparatus, instruments, and equipment world-wide. Thankfully, Bill, who had worked at Lab-Line for over 28 years and drove 104 miles round trip to work each day, and a few other "old-timers" were there to share their Lab-Line stories and memories about my father, mother, and better times with Jordan and me.

One of the "old-timers" was J. P. McSwain, who was startled when he saw me walking through the plant. "Mrs. Newman, Mrs. Newman," he called out to me.

"No, it's Sheila, J. P.," I responded.

"You look so much like your Mama, I thought I was seeing a ghost," J. P. replied.

J.P. wrapped his arms around me, and I wrapped mine around him. We both melted into a hug filled with memories of Lab-Line and my parents. J. P. told me how sad he was to be losing his job.

"Lab-Line has been my home since I was 18-years-old and your mother and father always treated me with dignity and respect," he reminisced before I made my way from the plant into the office and my father's library.

As expected, the library was perfectly intact with a treasury of his business, scientific, and Judaica books and memorabilia.

20

My father, a mechanical engineer, was a voracious reader. His familiar signature "Alexander I. Newman" was prominent on the inside cover of each book. We felt a sense of reverence and joy as we sorted through the shelves and carefully boxed our treasures.

As we were packing the last boxes, Mary Beth Rupert, the Human Resource Director, arrived in the library and offered me 2 old black cardboard three-ringed binders. "I thought you might want these," she said. At first, I wasn't sure why. However, when I saw the open end of the notebooks and gazed at the pastel pink, yellow, green, blue, and peach pages of the Lab-Line *HI-LITER*, I knew I was holding a precious archive. The notebooks were brimming with the last remnants of the Lab-Line *HI-LITER*, which was "an employee newspaper published by and for the employees of Lab-Line, Instruments, Inc." that employees, customers, family, and friends had enjoyed for many years.

I hugged Mary Beth and thanked her for rescuing such a significant and meaningful portion of my family's history. On the drive home, I began reading the content of the first notebook. I felt as if I had opened a time capsule.

When we arrived at home, I put the notebooks away for safe keeping on our son Noah's bookshelf, which I used for storage while he was working in Brazil. In October of 2008, I began re-organizing Noah's room. He had sold his business in Sao Paulo, Brazil, and he and his family were returning to Chicago and would live with us until he secured a job.

As I began re-arranging the bookshelves, the Lab-Line notebooks beckoned to me. When I took a break from my tasks, I began re-reading the notebooks.

Once again, the newsletters offered messages and memories of my family and the Lab-Line family that began with 2 determined individuals and grew to over 250 dedicated individuals, who worked together for 53 years.

From 2005 until 2016, my life was filled with the blessing of a thriving business, book publications, and family. Then in January of 2017, I realized that on March 5, 2017 Lab-Line would have celebrated its 65th year of business.

One again, I began reading through the *HI-LITER* newsletters' multi-colored pastel pages. The words resonated with a different relevance than they did previously. Now, technology had rapidly changed the world, cultures, business development, leadership styles, customer service, employee relationships, and product manufacturing. I realized that the sensible anecdotes and adages, mindful acknowledgements and advice, motivating stories and quotes, and news articles that were written by Lab-Line employees were still relevant and beneficial.

Just as my father recognized that his job was in jeopardy, he knew it was critical to explore ideas and formulate a plan to launch his own business. I knew it was the appropriate time to write and share my parents', Lab-Line's and the *HI-LITER* newsletters' inspiring stories with others.

I am grateful that I was exposed to my parent's tenacious entrepreneurship. My parents exemplified, encouraged, and shared the values of teamwork, loyalty, ethics, education, dedication, innovation, communication, fairness, inspiration, motivation, patriotism, appreciation, pride, integrity, consideration, and collaboration; which also filled the Lab-Line *HI-LITER* newsletters.

In 1953, Julia Amorella, my father's executive secretary, wrote the first company newspaper entitled Lablines. It included one of my father's "No Bunk" business principles: "The final judge is always the customer."

The first Lab-Line *HI-LITER* "newspaper" was written by the employee reporters on January 16, 1970. The following was written in the first copy:

"The Lab-Line *HI-LITER* is an employee paper, published bi-weekly by and for the employees of Lab-Line Instruments, Inc. and its subsidiaries at 15th and Bloomingdale Aves., Melrose Park, Illinois. Staff: Editor: L.E. Hardin; Reporters: Kay Smith, Newton Reed, J. P. McSwain, Alice Brown; and Typist: Karen Woodford." Future reporters were: Virginia Cangialosi, Ann Robbins, Roger Yates, Joan Burr, and Dorothy Samlow

The *HI-LITER* included news about the company, departments, employees, customers, dealers, and their family members. Lab-Line employment anniversaries, wedding anniversaries, birthdays, get well wishes, condolences, business advice, suggestions, recipes, family picnics, holiday greetings, business announcements and awards, and charity donations were also included.

As I was adding articles for the first chapter of the book, I realized that I had selected many Edgar A. Guest poems that my father had contributed to the Lab-Line *Hi-Liter* newsletter. Both my father and I appreciated and enjoyed Edgar A. Guest, who was known as the people's poet. We found merit and inspiration in his words and prolific works. In the March 15, 1968 Lab-Line *Hi-Liter* newsletter, I discovered the following poem that was contributed by my father. The poem is the fundamental essence of this book and how my father, along with my mother, used **No Bunk Truths** to build a thriving business, demonstrate exemplary leadership, encourage and care for dedicated employees, and offer authentic customer service to achieve and maintain Lab-Line's success!

My father, who was an old-fashioned man, wrote: "The following poem was written by one of America's outstanding poets, Edgar A. Guest, who passed away in 1959. The following story applied yesterday, it applies today, and it will apply as long the world is in existence."

Old Fashion Stuff
My father was an old-fashion man they said, with notions passed out of date,
He fancied the best way of getting ahead
Was to work and have patience to wait.
By practice, he told us, skill came to the hand,
From study comes learning, he'd say,
And it grieved him to think that the youth of the land
Could believe in an easier way.

"If it's roses you'd grow you must dig in the soil;
If you'd rule you must learn to obey;
If money you'd spend you must earn it by toil."
My father would frequently say,
"If a dollar you borrow, a dollar return;
Debt is something all honest men pay."
And it grieved him to think that his teachings we'd spurn
Or believe in an easier way.

Well, we've lived and we've laughed through the wisecracking age, and of smartness we've taken our fill.
We are ready, I think, to bring back to life's stage
Work, honesty, patience, and skill.
The start's at the bottom and not at the top
As my old-fashion father would say,

The way to the desk is to work in the shop
And there's never an easier way."

My Father did not remain at his desk. He made a practice of walking through his shop "plant" and speaking with the Lab-Line employees, referring to each individual by their name, which he made a point of knowing, and asking them about their job and their families.

Now, business owners, leaders, managers, and team members who need a blueprint for success can read and benefit from the Lab-Line *HI-LITER* newsletters. The values and methodologies that were relevant to building a competitive and successful business in the mid-20th century are still valid today. The wisdom in the Lab-Line *HI-LITER* newsletters previously enjoyed reverberating cheers and endured rigorous changes and challenges. Yet, their messages have remained visionary and long-lasting; and serve as the foundation of ***No Bunk, Just B. S. (Business Sense): 50 Timely and Timeless Truths Business School Cannot Teach You***!

It's comforting and enriching to know that the Lab-Line legacy and legend will continue to resonate and impact me, my family, and the Lab-Line alumni, as well as each individual who reads and shares ***No Bunk, Just B. S. (Business Senses): 50 Timely and Timeless Truths Business School Cannot Teach You!***

NO BUNK JUST BS (BUSINESS SENSE)

Chapter 1

Building a Thriving Business Truths

No Bunk, Just BS

The Founders

My father graduated from Armour Institute of Technology, now known as the Illinois Institute of Technology (IIT), in 1924 with a degree in mechanical engineering. He also enrolled in graduate business classes at Northwestern University in the evening after his day job and earned his master's degree in business. At that time, both were remarkable achievements for the third son of Eastern European Jewish immigrants.

My mother attended the School of the Art Institute of Chicago for fashion design after graduating high school in 1934. However, during the Great Depression she was not able to complete her education. She had a flair for fashion and could visualize a dress pattern and solve mathematical problems in her head. She became a fashionable entrepreneur, designing, sewing, and selling clothes to make financial contributions to her family.

After 13 years of marriage as life partners, my parents became business partners and our home life rapidly re-adjusted to their new partnership. At home and at "the plant," my parents were a consummate team. My mother's competent eye for design, mathematical aptitude, and business skills were a superb benefit to their partnership.

My father always said that my mother was his most knowledgeable, elegant, beautiful, and accomplished sales professional—especially when she accompanied him to laboratory industry trade shows, such as SAMA (Association of Scientific Apparatus Makers) and FSSAB (Federated Societies of Biological Sciences).where they displayed and took orders for Lab-Line's latest state-of-the-art equipment. During Lab-Line's infancy, my mother worked alongside my father, as they worked long hours to grow the business.

Our family dinner table discussions quickly began to focus on the new business. Often, our dining room became the Lab-Line "Personnel Office." My father would invite prospective employees home for dinner, and my mother the "Personnel Manager" would "size them up" with her unique interview process. She would prepare and serve a gourmet meal, then graciously query the dinner guests about their personal and professional life. Unbeknownst to them, they had just had their second interview. If my mother gave her "OK" they were hired. Sometimes my parents would disagree, and my mother would warn my father, "Al you're going to waste 6 months training him, and then you'll have to let him go." Ninety-nine percent of the time my father trusted my mother's analysis. It was that 1% when he didn't, that he regretted his decision. Mother was an intuitive and consistent judge of character.

Al and Sylvia Newman at Lab-Line's 25th anniversary party sharing acknowledgements, memories, and cake with employees, and celebrating everyone's contributions and successes, on March 5, 1977.

On March 30, 1977, Al and Sylvia Newman partnerships abruptly ended when my father died from a heart attack.

My parents had been devoted life partners for 39 years and successful business partners for 25 years.

Building a Thriving Business Truth #1

Follow Imperative Instructions to Build Your Business

The 10 Commandments of Business

1. Handle the hardest job first each day.

2. Do not be afraid of criticism—criticize yourself often.

3. Be glad and rejoice in other fellow's success and study his methods.

4. Do not be misled by dislikes. Acid ruins the finest fabrics; however, both may be used to advantage.

5. Be enthusiastic, it is contagious.

6. Do not have the notion that success means money-making.

7. Be fair, and do at least one decent act every day.

8. Honor the chief. There must be a head of everything.

9. Have confidence in yourself, believe you can do it.

10. Harmonize your work. Let the sunshine radiate and penetrate your relationships.

Building a Thriving Business Truth #2

Treat People With "Pleasant Words and Smiling Eyes"

Good Business (Edgar A. Guest, written in 1942)

If I possessed a shop or store, I'd drive the grouches off my floor!
I'd never let a gloomy guy offend the folks who come into buy
I'd never keep a boy or clerk with a mental toothache at his work,
Nor let a man who draws my pay drive customers of mine away.

I'd treat the man who takes my time and spends a nickel or a dime,
with courtesy and make him feel that I was pleased to close the deal
because tomorrow, who can tell? He may want stuff I have to sell,
and in that case, then he will be glad to spend all his dollars with me.

The reason people pass one door to patronize another store,
it is not because the business place has better silk, or gloves, or lace
or cheaper prices, but it lies in pleasant words and smiling eyes;
The only difference, I believe, is in the treatment folks receive.

Building a Thriving Business Truth #3

Encouragement Will Help to Grow Your Business

1966 New Year's Message to Everyone

With the coming of the New Year, everyone makes a certain number of New Year's resolutions. Some we keep, and some we break.

Let's make a few (at Lab-Line)! Let us all resolve:

1. To make our individual jobs a pleasure and an opportunity to demonstrate our individual abilities.

2. To improve the quality of our products.

3. To improve our customer service.

4. To improve our housekeeping in every department so we will be a model company for our customers to see... It is your home for 8 hours a day.

5. To submit your suggestions and receive your rewards.

6. To work together with one another, for the benefit of ourselves and our customers.

7. To not to be satisfied with what we are doing today, but to do better in 1966.

8. And, finally, let us resolve to make 1966 a banner year for yourselves, your family, and your company.

A HAPPY AND SAFE NEW YEAR!

A. I. Newman

Building a Thriving Business Truth #4

Be Adaptable!

That's What They Said ...

It seems to be that the key to our future can be summed up in one word: Adaptability. In a rapidly changing world, it is often a matter of survival to change one's mind, one's attitude, and one's way of thinking and doing things. Even when survival is not at issue, we should know how to adjust to changed circumstances in order to capitalize on new opportunities.

Building a Thriving Business Truth #5

People Make Things Happen

Four Kinds of People

There are four kinds of people in the world:

1. Those who **make** things happen.

2. Those to **whom** things happen.

3. Those who **watch** things happen.

4. Those who don't even **know** that things are happening.

Say to yourself, **"Who am I?"**

Building a Thriving Business Truth #6

How you Think Will Make a Difference

It's All In A State Of Mind
(Walter D. Wintle, published in 1905 by Unity Tract Society,
Unity School of Christianity)

If you think you are beaten, you are,
If you think you dare not, you don't,
If you like to win, but you think you can't,
It's almost a "cinch" you won't.

If you think you'll lose, you've lost,
For out in the world you find
Success begins with a fellow's will;
It's all in the state of mind.

Full many a race is lost
Ere ever a step is run;
And many a coward fails
Ere ever his work's begun.

Think big and your deeds will grow,
Think small and you'll fall behind,
Think that you can and you will;
It's all in the state of mind.

If you think you're outclassed, you are,
You've got to think high to rise,
You've got to be sure of yourself before
You can ever win a prize.

Life's battles don't always go
To the stronger or faster man,
But sooner or later, the man who wins,
Is the fellow who thinks he can.

Building a Thriving Business Truth #7

Take Pride in Your Work

Sign Your Name

Do you take enough pride in all your work to sign your name to it?

Write your signature on the line below:

_____

Building a Thriving Business Truth #8

Making Mistakes Can Make You Wiser

Plutarch's Advice (Lucius Mestrius *PLUTARCHUS* was a Greek biographer and essayist)

To make no mistakes is not in the power of man; but from their errors and mistakes the wise and good learn wisdom for the future.

Building a Thriving Business Truth #9

CANNOT Can Be More Instructive Than a CAN

10 CANNOTments

(adapted from William John Henry Boetcker in Lincoln
on Private Property; leaflet, 1916)

- YOU CANNOT create prosperity by discouraging thrift.

- YOU CANNOT strengthen the weak by weakening the strong.

- YOU CANNOT uplift small minded people by tearing down big minded people.

- YOU CANNOT uplift the meager by reducing the abundance.

- YOU CANNOT help wage earners by hurting wage payers.

- YOU CANNOT progress by spending more than your income.

- YOU CANNOT achieve security on borrowed money.

- YOU CANNOT attain brotherhood through class emphasis.

- YOU CANNOT build independence by dulling initiative.

- YOU CANNOT truly help others by doing for them what they could be doing for themselves.

Building a Thriving Business Truth #10

It Is Critical to Recognize the Difference Between a Winner and a Loser

How to Tell the Difference Between a Winner and a Loser

A **Winner** says, "I'm good, but not as good as I could be."
A **Loser** says, "I'm not as bad as a lot of other people."

A **Winner** respects those who are more skillful and tries to learn something from them.
A **Loser** resents those who are more skilled and tries to find their vulnerability.

When a **Winner** makes a mistake, he or she says, "I was wrong."
When a **Loser** makes a mistake, he or she says, "It wasn't my fault."

A **Winner** makes commitments.
A **Loser** makes promises.

A **Winner** offers explanations.
A **Loser** offer excuses.

A **Winner** feels responsible for his or her job.
The **Loser** says, "I only work here."

A **Winner** knows what to fight for and what to compromise.
A **Loser** fights for what is not worthwhile and compromises on what he or she should not.

A **Winner** says, "Let's find out!"
A **Loser** says, "Nobody knows!"

Are you a **Winner** or a **Loser**?

NO BUNK JUST BS

(BUSINESS SENSE)

Chapter 2

Exemplary Leadership Truths

A Memorable Leader

By 1948, my father recognized that his time at Precision Scientific was limited. It was a family business and family member returning from World War II would soon dominate the company leadership.

I clearly remember my mother telling me about the idea to start Lab-Line. "At that time, your father and I saw the handwriting on the wall," she recalled, "and we began making plans to start our own laboratory instrument and equipment business."

In 1951, my father gave his notice to Precision Scientific. My parents initiated their plans to begin Lab-Line with 3 employees; my father, my mother, and my father's loyal secretary Julia Amorella. When leaving Precision, my father's team members gave him a beautiful brass clock as a thank you gift—which now resides in an honored place in my home.

In 2001, my mother passed away. In her personal papers, I found the "A Goodbye Gift from All of Us" card that had accompanied the clock, with 35 names of the team who signed the card. Many of the signatures were men who later worked at Lab-Line and/or who became "business friends" of my parents. My mother saved the card after my father passed away in 1977. She also saved an astonishing, yellowed with time, letter written a year and a after my father left Precision Scientific.

"To: Mr. Walter W. Pitann, Chairman of the Board of Directors
We, the undersigned employees of PRECISION SCIENTIFIC COMPANY, have seen the company, over the past many years grow and become successful. Our jobs were secure and our morale was good. In general, conditions were satisfactory. All this was accomplished under the direction of Mr. A. I. Newman.

In the past year and a half, all this was changed. The new management has been wasteful and inefficient. Poor judgment has been shown everywhere. We feel our jobs are no longer safe and our future is in doubt.

We are discouraged and dissatisfied. We feel that our company has gone backwards and does not have the right kind of leadership. Morale is extremely low and the whole organization is in a state of confusion. We know that the company is losing money when other companies are making money. Our pensions will mean nothing to us. It is rumored that many of our suppliers do not want to sell to us, because we cannot not pay.

Our company must go ahead, and we feel it can only go ahead as it did in the past under the leadership of Mr. Newman. Put Mr. Newman back to lead us."

The letter was impressive because the employees risked their livelihoods to send it. What was more remarkable about the letter was the attached petition with 71 employees' signatures. Again, I recognized many of the signatures as individuals who left Precision Scientific in order to help my parents build Lab-Line

Exemplary Leadership Truth #1

Leaders Do Not Go it Alone

What Is Leadership?

LEADERS are a people who are going somewhere, but not going alone. They take others with them.

Their ability in setting up situations in which others are willing to follow them and are happy to work with them is a precious skill called Leadership.

This skill is made up of many qualities of thoughtfulness and consideration for others, enthusiasm, the ability to share responsibilities with others, and a multitude of other traits.

But fundamentally, Leaders are the one who leads, who have a plan, who keep headed toward a goal and a purpose.

They have the passion to keep moving forward in such a way that others gladly go with them.

Exemplary Leadership Truth #2

An Understanding Leader Practices Sincere Listening Skills

Listen Carefully

If you don't listen, you do not hear.

If you don't hear, you don't understand, you make mistakes, mistakes cost money, jobs, and sometimes lives.

I know you might believe you understand what you think I said.

But I am not sure you realize that what you heard is not what I meant.

Exemplary Leadership Truth #3

Mindful Leaders Know the Importance of the Words They Speak

5 Important Words

The five most important words are: "I am proud of you."

The four most important: "What is your opinion?"

The three most important: "If you please."

The two most important: "Thank you."

The least important: "I"

Exemplary Leadership Truth #4

An Excellent Leader Improves People's Lives

The Man of Real Excellence

The man whose sole pursuit is Profit and Advantage can be ruined by a bad harvest.

But a man whose sole pursuit is Excellence cannot be confused by bad times.

These are the 5 ways in which a man of real Excellence improves other people:

1. Some he transforms like rain in season.

2. Others he perfects excellence that already exists.

3. Others he brings success to innate capacity.

4. Others he provides answers to questions.

5. Others derive benefit in their own way.

To act without knowing why; to do things as they have always been done, without asking why; to engage in an activity all one's life without really understanding what it is about and how it relates to other things—this is to be one of the crowd, not a man of Excellence.

Exemplary Leadership Truth #5

Develop a Precise and Effective Mission Statement for Your Business

An Effective Mission Statement

The Lab-Line Mission Statement was printed in capital letters at the top of each *HI-LITER* newsletter. The statement demonstrates my father's detailed mechanical engineering perspective and skills.

The statement also spoke to his personal commitment and his company's promise to the employees, the customers, and the people whose lives would be saved by Lab-Line laboratory equipment and instruments.

The precise verbiage is significant, and the statement has lasted the test of time and rings true now, as it did when my father wrote it in 1952.

THE OBJECTIVE OF LAB-LINE SHALL BE TO PROVIDE THE SCIENTIST WITH THE BEST-MADE, BEST-PERFORMING, AND MOST MODERN INSTRUMENTS TO DO HIS WORK; TO PROVIDE JOBS AND JOB SECURITY FOR THOSE WHO APPLY THEMSELVES CONSISTENTLY AND EFFECTIVELY TO THEIR JOBS; AND TO MAKE A PROFIT TO CONTINUE ITS OPERATIONS AND MAINTAIN ITS OBJECTIVES.

Now you can fill in the blanks and personalize this statement for your own business Mission Statement.

THE OBJECTIVE OF _____

SHALL BE TO PROVIDE _____

WITH THE BEST-_____,

BEST-_____,

AND MOST _____

TO DO _____WORK;

TO PROVIDE _____

AND _____ SECURITY FOR

_____ WHO APPLY THEMSELVES

CONSISTENTLY AND EFFECTIVELY TO THEIR JOBS;

AND TO MAKE A PROFIT TO CONTINUE

_____ OPERATIONS AND

MAINTAIN _____ OBJECTIVES.

Exemplary Leadership Truth #6

A Compassionate Leader Cares for and Inspires Others

Thank You for my Second Chance!

Many people considered my father a "tough" man. Yes, he was tough on himself and those he cared about because he wanted them to succeed, feel safe, and learn how to take care of themselves and their loved ones. The following two stories exemplify my father's earnest, compassionate, courageous, and inspirational attributes, and how people proved their gratitude in return.

My father was a fair man. He was willing to give people a second chance if they demonstrated sincerity and commitment to their job. The following story demonstrates the earnestness of a Lab-Line employee.

The Christmas card was stamped "**RECEIVED DEC 16 1976 LAB-LINE INC**" on the back.

The front had a visual of brightly colored Christmas ornaments in a silver bowl, pine cones, and a red candle in a silver candlestick with an etched class hurricane glass.

The Greeting read: **To Some One SPECIAL at Christmas**. Inside was written a personal note to my father that was written three months before the he passed away.

"Dear Papa Newman, Thank you for giving me a second chance with my job. I hope never to change jobs with you being my boss. God bless all your family. You are very good to me. Obliged, Carmen Olivo"

Compliments and a Gift for a Great Leader

The following was written about my father and his leadership skills in a *HI-LITER* Newsletter in honor of his birthday and Lab-Line's 20th anniversary.

"The President of Lab-Line Instruments is, to me, one of the greatest. He has wisdom, knowledge, prestige, is very efficient, has sound judgement, and has will power, which is very important. If we accept his corrections and instructions, we will achieve outstanding workmanship and be top quality employees. This will help our company become the best.
Remember, a job well done is to have done it! Above all we must have faith in ourselves in whatever we do! All is well!

(I hope I still have a job after this column has been written.)"
Charlestine in the advertising department

"Many thanks to all the wonderful people at Lab-Line for all their good wishes, and also for the beautiful pair of gold cufflinks in honor of my 39th plus, and Lab-Line's 20th Anniversary!"

A. I. Newman

Exemplary Leadership Truth #7

A Leader is Not a Boss

Boss vs. Leader

The boss drives the team; the Leader coaches them.

The boss depends upon authority; the Leader on good will.

The boss inspires fear; the Leader inspires enthusiasm.

The boss says, "I will"; the Leader says, "We will!"

The boss assigns the tasks; the Leader sets the pace.

The boss says, "Get here on time"; the Leader gets there ahead of time.

The boss fixes the blame for the breakdown; the Leader fixes the breakdown.

The boss makes work a drudgery; the Leader makes it a game.

The boss says, "Go"; the Leader says, "Let's go!"

The world needs Leaders; but nobody wants a boss!

Exemplary Leadership Truth #8

A Collaborative Leader Knows a Team Working Together Gets the Job Done

When the Rooster Crows

When I was a young girl, I remember a boldly colored poster with a rooster crowing hanging outside my dad's office at home, Lab-Line's second home. It represented one of my father's leadership philosophies and attitudes.

Arthur S. Hollander, an early Lab-Line personnel manager, wrote a memo about people crowing about accomplishments.

"There's not a company in the world that is able to operate without one necessary ingredient—People! In any company that produces a tangible product, no one person can design that product, finance it, manufacture it, advertise it, and then deliver the merchandise to his customer himself. A company is people, working together as a team, helping each other along the way all for their own betterment.

At Lab-Line, there is no place for the person who is forever walking around, patting himself on the back, and crowing for all to hear about how the "Big I" is carrying all of the workload. One of the lost arts in today's world is the word "WE." Even at Lab-Line, what "WE" do together as a team is what really counts. Take a look at the sign in the cafeteria and remember what is says:

 **'Don't waste time blowing off about what can't be done or what you haven't done yet, get it done FIRST, then start to CROW!!'**

But when you do start to CROW, remember all of the **other** people who made your crowing possible!"

Exemplary Leadership Truth #9

Exemplary Leaders Measure Their Deeds with Rule and Square

Constructive Living

In an August 1973 *HI-LITER* newsletter, my father wrote the following column about expanding the size of the Lab-Line building:

Last week, on Thursday, August 16, 1973, we demolished the last of two old houses on our property. In one day, the house was leveled and soon the grass and weeds will take over and no will remember that on this ground once stood a house, lived in by many families over 50 years.

One could not help but feel a sense of remorse without thinking that what make man creates, man destroy. Many skilled workmen, working many months, built the home; but it took only a mechanical bulldozer less than a day to destroy.

As I watched, I could not help but recall a beautiful story written many years ago, entitled *Constructive Living*, which reads as follows:

Constructive Living
I stood on the streets of a busy town,
Watching men tearing a building down.
With a ho, heave ho, and a lusty yell,
They swung a beam—and a side wall fell!

I asked a foreman of the crew,
"Are those men as skilled as those
You'd hire if you wanted to build?"
"Ah, no" he said, "no, indeed,
Just common laborer is all I need.

I can tear down as much in a day or two
As it would take skilled men a year to do."
And then I thought as I went on my way,
Just which of these two roles am I trying to play?

Have I walked life's road—with care;
Measuring each deed with rule and square,
Or am I one of those who roams the town,
Content with the labor of—tearing down?

Exemplary Leadership Truth #10

An Intuitive Leader Recognizes What is Best for the Company

What's Best for the Organization, Is Best for You!

In a memo to Lab-Line employees, my father wrote: "The following story appeared recently, and since I feel it has plenty of merit, I wanted to share my feelings as to what the author has said. Many of the thoughts expressed apply not only to our company, but too many companies throughout the country. If you find situations of the type the author has described in your department, I hope that you will do something about it."

- Humans, on occasion, can be mature, reasonable, and cooperative. They can also be the exact opposite.

- There are always honest differences of opinion about how to get the job done. Also, those gray areas between functions are where responsibilities overlap, create friction, and lend fuel to personal jealousies. In addition to these natural obstacles to peaceful coexistence there is a third: a certain number of overly-aggressive individuals primarily concerned with building and protecting their own personal image.

- Given these ingredients, it is easily possible to mix up a stew wherein many people in the organization are spending more time and effort fighting each other than doing their jobs and fighting the competition—and getting customers.

- Everyone, from top to bottom should recognize certain facts:
  1. The welfare of your company and its customers come first.

2. Teamwork and cooperation will produce better results than fighting.
3. Personal ambitions, jealousies, or animosities must not interfere with what is best for the company and the customer.
4. Once a decision has been reached, the ranks must close, and everyone do his best to make it work.

- Everyone connected with a business is riding the same horse and a horse can't go in different directions at the same time. The person with real potential recognizes this almost instinctively. He develops the ability to rise above petty rivalries, to discount his personal feelings, and to do what he knows is best for the organization and the customer; and in the long run, himself.

A. I. Newman

No Bunk, Just BS

NO BUNK
BUNK
JUST BS
(BUSINESS SENSE)

Chapter 3

Employee and Teamwork Truths

Gratitude at Our Front Door

I can still recreate the peculiarly vivid scene of peering out the passenger window on the driver's side of our 1948 maroon Buick. It was a warm day and the driver's window was rolled down. I was leaning forward against the fuzzy beige wool upholstery, on the back of my father's seat. As we drove up our red brick driveway approaching our house, I wondered why there was a bundle of bright iridescent colors on the red brick porch below the white louvered screen door.

"Daddy, what are all those colors?" I asked my father.

"I'm not sure, let's take a look." He replied.

My father continued up the driveway and parked the car in front of our garage. Then my father, mother, and I curiously scrambled out of the car. To our surprise, we discovered a flock of dead pheasants perfectly laid out on our front porch. It was a puzzling and peculiar display because we did not know where they had come from, nor did we find an accompanying note.

"Al, why are there dead pheasants lying at our front door?" I remember my mother asking.

My father's response was another question. "Remember we had a Lab-Line employee who asked me for help because his young son was suffering from a rare type of cancer?"

"Yes." My mother replied.

I also remembered listening to my father phoning his contacts and customers at hospitals and universities laboratories, doctor offices, and businesses, to acquire an expensive experimental cancer drug for the employee's critically ill son.

My father had given us his solution to the pheasant mystery. The employee he helped was an avid hunter. The hunter had deposited the flock of pheasants at our front door to show his gratitude for my father's generosity and kindness to purchase the experimental cancer drug that saved his young son's life.

Employee and Teamwork Truth #1

Employees are Part-Owners of a Business

Hire a Winner

The type of employees that make the most progress are the ones who tackle their work with as much genuine interest and enthusiasm as though they were part-owners of the business. When we spot that kind of spirit in an employee, we know we've hired a winner. They are the most valuable people!

Employee and Teamwork Truth #2

Some Employees Are People of Consequence and Others Are Lightweights

Loyalty

If you work for a man—In heaven's name work for him. Speak well of him and stand by the institution he represents. Remember... loyalty is worth more than cleverness.

If you must condemn, undermine, and eternally find fault; resign your position. When you are out of the organization, damn to your heart's content.

But as long as you are part of an organization, do not condemn it. If you do, the first high wind that comes along will blow you away and you will never know why.

Employee and Teamwork Truth #3

Employees Deserve and Appreciate Recognition

Lab-Line Acknowledgements

I always looked forward to and loved reading the acknowledgements of the Lab-Line employees in the bi-monthly *HI-LITER* newsletters. Below are examples of Lab-Line employee recognitions:

1. The Holiday Lab-Line Honor Roll: "The Holiday Season is a time for joyful thankfulness. As Lab-Line reflects upon the past, we are acutely aware of those who have helped bring us to this place in our company's history. LAB-LINE is still a young and growing company. It is only little more than 15 years old and 200 strong. But the mere fact that we have honored 46 employees who have devoted so many of their working years, from 15 years or more to 5 years or more, emphasizes a very strong conclusion... LAB-LINE MUST BE A GOOD PLACE TO WORK!!!"

2. The monthly "We Proudly Salute" or "We're Completely Dedicated" articles: In recognition of the many years of service and devotion, Lab-Line Instruments acknowledges its appreciation of the following employees whose work anniversary is celebrated in (the month) with 2 or more years of service

3. Happy Birthdays, Wedding Congratulations, Happy Wedding Anniversaries, New Employee Welcome Messages, Baby Birth Announcements, and Retirement Best Wishes, Get Well Wishes, and Sincere Condolences.

4. Employee of the Month recognition always included fascinating information.

5. Monthly Perfect Attendance acknowledgements demonstrated employees' commitment to their jobs.

6. ***Kay's Comments:*** Kay Smith, a *HI-LITER* reporter, wrote about the Employees' Activity Club. The club was established for the purpose of developing and maintaining employee fellowship for all employees through athletics (a baseball team), social events, music, and other such activities that the club wished to sponsor. The club was run by the employees, for the employees.

7. ***Kay's Comments***: Kay Smith also wrote about a group of office and plant employees called the Communication Committee. The purpose of the group was to have conversations, talks and dialogue about how to improve the company, teamwork, working conditions and environment, and customer relations.

Other acknowledgements were from employees who were proud that Lab-Line was their only job. Many individuals had worked for Lab-Line for over 35 years. Many even drove a 90+ mile one way to work for years because they knew Lab-Line appreciated them.

Employee and Teamwork Truth #4

Employees Can Fall in Love with Their Jobs

You Say You Love Me (by Vera Hartke, a Lab-Line employee)

You say you love me but sometimes you don't show it. In the beginning you could not do enough for me. Now you seem to take me for granted. Some days I wonder if I mean anything at all to you.

Maybe when I'm gone, you'll appreciate me and all the things I do for you. I'm responsible for getting the food on your table, for your clean shirt, for the welfare of your children…a thousand and one things you want and need.

Why if it were not for me you wouldn't even have a car. I've kept quiet and waited to see how long it would take for you to realize how much you really need me.

Cherish me… take good care of me… and I will continue to take good care of you!

Who am I? **I am your job!**

Employee and Teamwork Truth #5

Employees Can Teach Teamwork and How to be a Valuable Employee

An Employee's Do's and Don'ts

I, as a Lab-Line employee have learned, and am still learning, while working with this company. After doing my work, these are some of the questions I ask myself. They could be of some help to many people:

1. Is it neat?

2. Is it clear?

3. Is it well done?

4. Have I put forth every effort to do my best?

5. Am I trying to do my best?

6. Am I doing my best to get to work on time?

7. Do I follow instructions?

While being here, these are a few points I try to practice:
1. Don't ever deliberately make someone feel small, humble, self-conscious, or distressed.

2. Don't say bluntly, "That's wrong." You will get along much better with your co-workers if you learn to say, "Don't you think it would be much better if it was done this way?"

3. Don't criticize your fellow workers in public.

4. Don't put the blame for your mistakes on someone else.

5. Don't be a bluffer or a show-off.

6. Don't go over your immediate supervisor's head.

7. Don't take liberties. Abide by the rules and regulations of the company.

8. Don't always take the credit yourself, learn to say WE instead of I.

9. Don't always be the fault-finder or chronic complainer.

10. Don't resent criticism. Welcome it, if it is good judgement. It will make you wiser and can be of great help to all of us .

11. Don't take a negative approach or attitude concerning your work. Always say, "Yes, I will try and do it." Think positively, always. By doing this you will gain more self-confidence.

12. Don't hesitate to ask questions if you are not sure of what you are doing.

13. Take special care to be modest about the qualities you possess, they are already recognized. Remember the credit which others give you is always greater than bragging about yourself.

These are only a few of the things I have learned while working at Lab-line, and I am still learning more.

Employee and Teamwork Truth #6

Employees Can Broaden Their Knowledge to Become More Valuable

How to Succeed in Business by Trying

On August 30, 1968, J. A. Chitwood (who was the Lab-Line personnel director at the time) wrote the follow memo to the Lab-Line employees, that remains valuable advice today.

If you were to list the characteristics of a successful Lab-Line employee, you would probably put down intelligence, job knowledge, good performance, determination, resourceful, courage, and dependability. All good employees possess these attributes.

In the wear and tear of competitive employment, character traits are usually quickly revealed. As a result, Lab-Line supervisors are apt to have a clear idea which of their employees could move to higher responsibilities, and which should remain where they are.

Unfortunately, most of us do not possess much objectivity when it comes to seeing ourselves as we appear to others. So it is not surprising when someone else gets promoted that we ask, "Why was I passed over?"

To answer this question, any employee who expects to move ahead must demonstrate the following essential qualities:

1. **He or she must have a thorough grasp of his or her own job**. Show by your performance that you can master any increased responsibilities.

2. **He or she must have a capacity for growth**. The individual who becomes so absorbed in his or her own work that he or she fails to see the assignment in relation to Lab-Line's total team effort stifles his or her own development.

3. **Check your own job competence**. Promotions seldom happen to a person who is doing mediocre work.

4. **Check your attitude**. To move ahead, you cannot disregard or ignore the activities of other Lab-Line departments. Be intensely proud of your department and your job, but always keep in mind that their function is only part of the whole. By themselves, either would not exist.

5. **Check your human relations skills.** People are the name of the game at Lab-Line. They are the "big pay-off." Being able to work pleasantly and cooperatively with colleagues, and the knack of knowing how to secure and keep respect and trust, are the "door openers" to broader opportunities and success.

Finally, if you are promoted to a supervisory position, you will be required to direct other employees' efforts to the attainment of Lab-Line's goals. You will require employee support to assure success. Learn to understand people!

But don't stop there! Enlarge your horizons by reading widely. Be aware of the economic, social, and political factors that affect Lab-Line.

The broader your knowledge, the more valuable you will become!

Employee and Teamwork Truth #7

Tell Employees "Thank You for a Good Job!"

You ARE Appreciated

Sometimes, it might seem to you as you go about your job, day to day, dependably and efficiently, that nobody ever notices.

Perhaps you seldom miss a day of work because of sickness or any other reason, but you wonder if anyone is paying attention to your attendance record.

Maybe you see careless work going on around you at times, and perhaps you doubt that anyone ever notices that you are careful.

If you're doing a good, solid job, and you're hard working and dependable and honest—DON'T WORRY, YOU ARE APPRECIATED!

Bosses and supervisors are human too, and sometimes they forget to pat you on the back when you're consistently doing a good job. They tend to devote most of their time and attention to trouble spots; and if you're not a trouble spot, then they are grateful they don't have to forever be checking up on you.

Your job performance is observed and recorded. You will be recognized for doing a good job when the chips are down.

So when you get the feeling that no one cares, remember that Lab-Line is watching and Lab-Line does care, Lab-Line appreciates you—even though Lab-Line many not always remember to say **"Thanks for Good Job!"**

Employee and Teamwork Truth #8

Let Your Employees Know You Care About and Respect Them

Who Cares About You?

In 1968, the business world can be seem coldblooded, heartless, cruel, ruthless, and only want out of employees what it can get. Business can forget to respect its employees as human beings. Lab-Line does care about its people, its employees. You, your family, and coworkers are important to us. At Lab-Line there is a definite feeling of "belonging," a sense of being an individual and knowing you are appreciated. There is much visual evidence that your company cares about YOU!

As an example, Mrs. Mary Roddan, a 13-year veteran of our Assembly Department, retired last week. Some companies may merely have wished her well and then forgotten her. Certainly no top official would have cared or, perhaps, even known.

But at Lab-Line, with relatively little fan-fare about it, our president A.I. Newman personally talked with Mary about her future, her plans, and spoke knowingly of her work in the Assembly Department. Then, as a final gesture, he presented her with an 18-inch television set to enjoy in her new life.

This was not something special. *Any* employee who reaches retirement age and who deserves to retire, and who has had ten years or more of consecutive employment at Lab-Line, will be awarded the same courtesies.

Employee and Teamwork Truth #9

Encourage Employees to Make Suggestions and Then Reward Them

How to Think Up Good Suggestions

1. Think about things that are wasted.
   How could the company cut down on waste?

2. Think about the reasons for each of the things you do.
   Is there a better way to get the same results?

3. Think about the size of things.
   Would a smaller size save material, money, or time?
   Would a larger size work better or last longer?

4. Think about the customer.
   How could you and/or our company satisfy the customer better?
   How could our company improve products or services?

5. Think about time?
   How could time be saved?

6. Think about errors or mistakes.
   Why did they happen?
   How could they be prevented?

7. Think about your work
   What is boring, tiring, or difficult?
   How could it be made more interesting, energizing, or easier?

8. Think about safety.
   How might someone be hurt?
   How could that be prevented?

9. Think about our problems.
   What solutions could you offer?

10. Think about things that are done "the same old way."
    Is that activity still necessary?
    Is it still the best way?

11. Think about ideas that have worked for someone else.
    How could they be applied in your job?
    How could they be used in our company?

12. Think about how our company spends its money.
    Would you spend your money that way?
    How could the company save money?

Why not use the suggestion box? Good suggestions pay off!
No individual has all the good ideas. Let's put our ideas to work.
Please put your suggestion on a piece of paper and place it in the
conveniently located suggestion box. Each suggestion will receive
serious consideration. Awards consist of: Excellent = $15.00,
Good = $10.00, Fair = $5.00. Think about methods, materials,
increasing sales, work conditions, and office procedures. Your
ideas will benefit us in 3 ways:

1. Lab-Line saves money.

2. We help insure our jobs.

3. You can make some extra money that will be included in your paycheck.

Suggestions were numbered and written out by the personnel department, now referred to as the human resources department, and then they were acknowledged and published in the *HI-LITER* newsletter. The following are examples:

1. Suggestion #14899: On our sheet metal patterns we mark down what the bend is supposed to be next to the bend line, because the bend lines can be off 1/32". Very good suggestion! This will be done by the Group Leader of the brakes at the time the job is being set up. A reward of $10.00 to Tim Geminn who submitted this prior to being promoted to Foreman.

2. Suggestion #3446: Purchase a portable lift truck for use in the Assembly Department. Good thinking. However, for the amount of time Assembly uses a fork lift, it would not pay.
Sorry, try again.

Employee and Teamwork Truth #10

Each Employee and Their
Job is Important to the Company

Your Job

Wherever you're working, in office or shop,
and however far you may be from the top,
and though you may think you're treading the mill,
don't ever belittle the job that you fill.

For however little your job may appear,
you're just as important as some little gear
that fits with others in a big machine that keeps it going,
though it is never seen.

And don't ever think you're of little account,
remember, you're part of the total amount.
If we didn't need you,
you would not be here,
so always keep you chin in the air.

A digger of ditches, mechanic, or clerk,
think well of your company, yourself, and your work.

NO BUNK JUST BS (BUSINESS SENSE)

Chapter 4
Customer Service and Care Truths

The Mysterious Little Brown Cardboard Box

It was the spring of 1961 and my mother was recovering from experimental lung surgery to cure her Tuberculosis. When I returned from school my mother asked me if I would drive her on an errand for my father. I was excited to be her chauffer because I had recently acquired my driver's license and loved any reason to drive.

We lived in River Forest, which is a suburb 11 miles west of downtown Chicago, and traffic was not as congested as it is now. I drove my mother to South Michigan Avenue and 12th Street, which was shabby area at that time. I made a U-turn and parked on the east side of the street, as my mother requested. She pointed out a dilapidated office building across the street and said, "I am going into that building and will be back in a few minutes. Lock the doors."

I locked the car doors and watched her walk across the street to the dilapidated office building. Ten minutes later, I was relieved to see my mother emerged from the building. She was protectively holding a little brown cardboard box in her hands. She safely crossed the street and returned to the passenger seat of our car. Then she looked at me and instructively said, "Sheila, we were never here."

I unquestioningly replied, "Yes, mother, we were never here."

As we drove home we chatted about school and my friends, but we did not discuss the little brown cardboard box that my mother was protectively holding in her lap.

When we arrived home, my mother put the little brown cardboard box on the hat shelf in my father's coat closet in our foyer.

When my father arrived home I was eager to hear what he had to say about the box. All he said was, "Sylvia, did you get the package?"

"It is on the hat shelf in your coat closet, Al." My mother replied.

Nothing was mentioned about the little brown cardboard box at dinner. The next morning, I ate breakfast with my father, but nothing was said about the secret on his hat shelf. As my father prepared to leave for his office before I left for school, he removed his hat, coat, and the little brown box from his coat closet. He kissed my mother and me good-bye and went out the front door, protectively holding the little brown cardboard box.

The mysterious little brown cardboard box was not mentioned again until 1967. My parents had invited Mr. and Mrs. Lehr, who were business customers and friends to my wedding. After the wedding my husband, my parents, and I were relieved and delighted that Mr. Lehr had also brought his camera and took many special photos that the professional photographer missed.

A few weeks after the wedding, we all looked through pictures that Mr. Lehr sent. I was surprised when my mother said, "Your father and I were thrilled that Mr. and Mrs. Lehr were able to attend your wedding for another reason besides taking these photos."

Then she paused and said, "Do you remember the errand to pick up the little brown cardboard box when you were a sophomore in high school?"

"Of course I remember the errand, the little brown cardboard box, and you telling me we were never there." I replied.

"Would you like to know what was in the box?" My mother teased.

"Absolutely!" I answered.

"That little brown cardboard box contained experimental (not yet approved by the FDA) breast cancer medicine," my mother explained. "Your father was able purchase the medicine from that company on Michigan Avenue because they used our Lab-Line equipment. After we picked up the medicine, you father shipped it to Mr. and Mrs. Lehr; it was the cure for Mrs. Lehr's breast cancer, which saved her life!"

Customer Service and Care Truth #1

Your Customers Will Judge
How Well You Have Treated Them

The Judge

My father's Customer Service credo:

"The final judge is always the customer!"

Customer Service and Care Truth #2

Provide Your Customer with
Quality Care, Service, and Products!

A. I. Newman's Lab-Line Quality Quotes

1. "The customer is our boss, treat him right!"

*2. "Satisfying the customers is our most important job…
and yours!"*

*3. "The life you save at Lab-Line, may be your own. Build it
better!"*

*4. "Our main objective should always be new products and the
best of service and product quality."*

Customer Service and Care Truth #3

Customers Are of Greatest Importance, Treat Them with Appreciation

A Customer

A Customer:
Is the most important person in any business.
Is not dependent on us, we are dependent on him.

A Customer:
Is not an interruption of our work, he or she is the purpose of it.
Does us a favor when he or she calls, we are not doing him a favor by serving him.
Is part of our business, not an outsider.
Is not a cold statistic, he is a flesh and blood human being with feelings and emotions like our own.

A Customer:
Is not someone to argue or match wits with.
Is a person who brings us his or her wants, it is our job to fill those wants.
Is deserving of the most courteous and attentive treatment we can give him or her.
Is the man or woman who makes it possible to pay your salary, whether you work in the stockroom, sales department, or the office.

A Customer:
Is the life-blood of this and every other business!

Customer Service and Care Truth #4

Customers Want the "Best" Customer Services and Products

A Note From the *HI-LITER* Editor

We recently received a letter of inquiry from one of our customers who stated in part:

"Dear Sirs,
We are informed that your company is one of the best designers and manufacturers of scientific instruments in the country."

This portion of the letter makes me think:
1. Is it really true?
2. Are we really the best?
3. Could we be the best?
4. Can you prove to yourself that we are the best?
5. Can you prove to our customers that we are the best?

Which category do you think we fall into?

Customer Service and Care Truth #5

Customers Will Remember
Your Company's Excellent Reputation

1. My Primary Choice

I was astonished when my friend Caryn told me, "When I was doing medical research in the 1950's and 1960's at Michael Reese Hospital and the University of Illinois in Chicago, I was in charge of purchasing all our lab equipment. Lab-Line was my primary choice because everything I purchased worked so well and for so long that replacements were usually unnecessary. Working with the company was facilitated by a sales representative who discerned what my needs were and cared enough to marry their equipment with my current and future needs."

Caryn Amster, author of *The Pied Piper of South Shore: Toys and Tragedy in Chicago*

2. The Best Equipment Available

Several years ago, I attended a book club meeting where we discussed the ***Immortal Life of Henrietta Lacks***. A guest microbiologist Dr. Stewart Lipman elaborated on the scientific discoveries in the book. I couldn't help but notice that Dr. Lipman often commented on the laboratories and equipment mentioned in the book and that he also used for his own research. I was curious to know about the equipment he used in his laboratory.

After the book discussion, I asked him, "Are you familiar with Lab-Line Instruments?"

His grateful expression morphed to surprise, as he responded, "Yes, of course. I still have Lab-Line equipment in my laboratory.

It was the most expensive equipment, but the best equipment available."

I joyfully replied, "I am delighted to hear your compliments because my parents were Al and Sylvia Newman, the founders and owners of Lab-Line!"

Dr. Lipman was shocked by my response. Then he continued to extol Lab-Line's excellent status in the industry. It was gratifying to know that Lab-Line's excellent reputation was still appreciated.

Customer Service and Care Truth #6

Customers and Service Providers Will Appreciate That You Value and Treat Them as Loyal Friends

Even a Dog Remembers

Many of my parents' dearest friends were individuals they met because of Lab-Line. Those friends began as customers, distributors/dealers of Lab-Line equipment, medical researchers and doctors, and suppliers and material, equipment, and service providers, such as their attorneys and accountant.

Extraordinary individuals, many who supported my parents from the first days of Lab-Line, were "business" friends who also became personal friends. Those friendships spanned decades; my parents remembered and cherished each one.

Below is an anecdote my father, a dog lover, wrote for the *HI-LITER* newsletter about friendship.

"Driving west on the Eisenhower expressway, one day, I saw a dog lying in the gutter killed by a passing motorist some time earlier. Sitting patiently besides the dead dog was his pal, another dog, hoping, I presume, that his friend would come to life. He was sitting there in the blazing morning sun mourning the death of his friend. Even a dog knows. Even a dog remembers.

But do human beings know the value of a real friend? Are they fair weather friends, good time Charlies, and when the wheel of fortune turns do they run away?

When a friend needs a helping hand, do they extend theirs or do they climb back into their shells and say, "too bad; it's his hard luck."

That's not a real friend that is just an acquaintance.

We all have loads of acquaintances, but just a handful of real friends with whom we share our pains and our pleasures, our sorrows, and our misfortunes. Just as sunshine follows rain, so do our real friends remember us and stand beside us in good times and bad.

Even a dog remembers and stands, forever, besides his friend."

Customer Service and Care Truth #7

Reward Your Business Partners with Excellent Customer Service

Recognition

Sargent-Welch is one of Lab-Line's major dealers. They just completed their national sales meeting where Alexander I. Newman, Bill Keef, and Ken Hopkins were invited to present a series of eight training seminars.

Everyone was very impressed with Lab-Line's products and presentation. The theme of the meeting was "Partners in Profit," expressing the company's desire to work more closely with their suppliers.

Lab-Line was honored to receive a bronze plaque in recognition of our close cooperation and excellent customer service with Sargent-Welch. This plaque is proudly displayed in the cafeteria, since it was all of you that earned it.

Customer Service and Care Truth #8

Always Give Customers Your Best Service

Our Customers Make the Big Decisions

1. Our customers are our bosses and **decide** if we get the job!

2. Our customers pay our wages by **deciding** to buy our goods and services!

3. Our customers determine our success by **deciding** to give us additional work!

Our customers want their money's worth and we must **decide** to always give our customers our best!

The following appeared on the front page of a *HI-LITER*:
THE GOOD WORD: The following is a copy of a letter which was recently received from Matheson Scientific, who is one of our distributors. I wanted to share it with all of you.

Dear Al,

In January we showed the Lab-Line/Matheson Scientific blue oven to our division managers. They were ecstatic! The design, construction, paint job, and all-over appearance pleased them a great deal.

Everyone who has seen the oven has been extremely impressed with the outstanding job that your employees have done in putting this package together for us. The attention to detail that your people have is definitely appreciated.

All of us here at Matheson have enjoyed working with everyone involved in this project. Your people have gone the 'extra step,' which is so important to supplying our customers with quality merchandise.

We at Matheson are proud that Lab-Line manufactures the Matheson Scientific oven.

Very truly yours,

MATHESON SCIENTIFIC, Gerald A. Cooney, Vice President of Marketing

Customer Service and Care Truth #9

Customers Need an Incentive to Continue a Relationship with You

I Am Your Customer

I am sensitive, especially when I am spending my money.

Whatever my personal habits may be, you can be sure of this:
I am a real nut on the type of service I receive.

If I detect signs of carelessness, unkept promises, poor quality,
poor packing of a shipment, ill manners or misconduct, I will take
my business elsewhere.

I am your customer now, but you must continue to prove that
selecting you was a wise move in the first place.

If I should ever criticize your service, take heed.
I do not dream up displeasure.

Let's find the source of the problem and eliminate it so that we can
continue to remain business friends.

Provide the incentive for me to continue to do business with you
and I will!

Customer Service and Care Truth #10

Reward Your Service Providers
for Excellent Customer Care

Surprise Gifts

When we completed our new building in September of 1963, we presented our general contractor, Mr. Gus Eifrig, and his architect, Mr. Fred Dolke, each with a gift for a job well done.

Both these men were surprised and delighted because this had never happened to them before. Usually it is the supplier who gives the gift to the customer. In this case we were the customer, and the architect and the general contractor were the supplier and the gifts were presented to them.

A. I. Newman

No Bunk, Just BS

NO BUNK JUST BS (BUSINESS SENSE)

Chapter 5

Achieving and Maintaining Success Truths

Job Security and Success

When circumstances forced my father to start over again, he not only built a new career, he built a successful business. This business became the largest in the laboratory, apparatus, instrument, and equipment business the industry. Lab-Line provided, as the mission statement said, "jobs and job security for those of our employees who apply themselves consistently and effectively to their jobs."

People often described my father as "stern." However, his corrective criticism was not meant to squash people and/or their ideas, but to challenge and encourage individuals to raise themselves to a higher level to be successful. Family and friends knew they could count on Al Newman's assistance for a job.

When our cousin, Angie (Ann) Robbin, was thirty-eight years of age, her husband, Jack, died suddenly. Ann unexpectedly was a widow. She needed job security to support my cousins, David, Barbara, and Linda. My father created a job for her as a secretary in the Engineering department. Angie diligently worked at her secretarial job from 1957 until 1980, when she retired.

Ann became the "Recipe Reporter" when she told my father, "I think we should have recipes in the newsletter." My father said, "OK, it's up to you to do it." Ann's "Culinary Corner" recipes were delicious contributions to the *HI-LITER* and her work ethic and dedication were valued contributions to Lab-line's success!

Achieving and Maintaining Success Truth #1

Worthwhile Work Creates Success

Success is Not Instant. Success in Anything Worthwhile Cannot be Ordered by Law; It Has to be Earned by Long, Hard, Intelligent Work.

1. Stature cannot be reached by demand; it has to be deserved.

2. Equality can only come from being equal; try to seize it and you will seize empty air.

3. Acceptance comes from being accepting.

4. Respect results from being respectful.

Achieving and Maintaining Success Truth #2

A Successful Business is Powered by Vitality

Vitality

Vitality is the power a business generates that will assure its success and progress, tomorrow.

Achieving and Maintaining Success Truth #3

Your Character Qualities Will Help You Succeed

How to Succeed in Business Without Trying

For anyone to move ahead and achieve success, he or she must demonstrate the following essential qualities:

1. **A thorough grasp of your job**. Show by performance that you are capable of mastering increased responsibilities.

2. **A capacity and a desire for growth**. Individuals who become so absorbed in their own work that they fail to see their assignments in relationship to their team efforts, stifle their own development.

3. **An understanding of their own competence**. Promotions seldom come to a person who is doing mediocre work.

4. **An awareness of others**. To move ahead, individuals cannot disregard or ignore the activities of other company departments. Be intensely proud of your department and your job; but always keep in mind that your contributions are only part of the whole and could not exist alone.

5. **Check your human relations skills**. People are the name of the game. They are the "big pay-off." Being able to work pleasantly and cooperatively with associates, and the knack of knowing how to secure and keep respect and trust, are the "door openers" to broader opportunities and success.

6. **Increase your knowledge**. Enlarge your horizon by reading widely. Be aware of the economic, social, and political factors that affect your company. The more you know the more valuable and successful you will become!

Achieving and Maintaining Success Truth #4

Success in Life Depends on the Motive

On November 11, 1966 my father made the following contribution to the *HI-LITER* Newsletter:

There is an old fable about a dog that boasted of his ability as a runner. One day he chased a rabbit, but failed to catch it. The other dogs ridiculed him. He replied, "Remember, the rabbit was running for his life, and I was running only for the fun of it."

Success in life depends on the motive. If you are in the race merely for the fun of it, or as a meal ticket, you will not put the same energy into your running as you will if your ambition is deeper and more serious.

I thought you would be interested in what the author had to say. Every once in a while all of us should sit down and ask ourselves:

- Am I putting into my job the best I can?

- Am I doing my best to make more happy and satisfied customers?

- Am I giving my job all I've got?

You will feel better if you do.

A. I. Newman

Achieving and Maintaining Success Truth #5

Have Confidence in Yourself

Every Individual Should Possess It

The one outstanding trait of every successful individual, whatever their business or profession should be, is confidence in themselves. Their opinions of others may vary, but one thing that never falters is the conviction they have about what they, themselves, can do.

They are certain that they can accomplish anything to which they put their mind and skills. They not only have faith, but the courage to back it up. They waste no time worrying about what others may think or say; nor do they listen long to the doubts and fears of the timid ones.

They make their own bold decisions, set a mark for themselves that is reasonable to attain, and never doubts their ability to reach it. Without confidence in themselves, an individual may never attract opportunity; and without opportunity, they cannot prove their worth.

Achieving and Maintaining Success #6

Do Not Underestimate Your Abilities

Measuring Success

Overestimating your ability may result in some disappointing realizations, but underestimating it can result in downright failure.

In the final analysis you should not measure your success by what you accomplished, but by what you can still accomplish.

Achieving and Maintaining Success Truth #7

Loyal and Responsible Employees Will Create Business Success

The Responsible One

The secret of a successful business is loyal employees who feel a personal responsibility to help it succeed.

"Lab-Line is grateful to the kind of employees who take this kind of interest. May we congratulate the following employees celebrating their employee anniversary this month, with 5 years or more, of service with Lab-Line." The employees' years of employment ranged from 20 to 6 years.

Achieving and Maintaining Success Truth #8

Follow 5 Simple Rules to
Climb the Ladder of Success

Five Steps to the Top

Do you want your climb to the top to be faster than it has been so far? By following a few simple rules, you can better your chances for success.

The first requirement is that you have to have ambition. Learn everything you can about your work, and always be willing to broaden your horizons.

Next, become a true professional by setting your goals high and learning the art of self-reliance.

Your third step is to communicate effectively by putting your ideas into a clear language.

A fourth and most important item is thoroughness. Cover every side of a question and follow every lead.

Finally, you will do best if you set a definite goal for yourself and keep it firmly in mind as you do your work.

Before you know it you may find the ladder of success stretching out below you instead of rising ominously in front of you.

Achieving and Maintaining Success Truth #9

Success is Built on Relationships

Meet the Success Family

The father of Success is Work.

The mother of Success is Ambition.

The eldest son is Common Sense.

His brothers are: Perseverance, Honesty, Thoroughness, Foresight, Cooperation, and Enthusiasm.

The eldest daughter is Character.

Her sisters are: Cheerfulness, Loyalty, Care, Economy, Sincerity, Harmony, and Courtesy.

The baby is Opportunity.

Become well acquainted with the father of the family and you develop a successful relationship with the entire family

Achieving and Maintaining Success Truth #10

Success Can Enrich Many Lives

How to Succeed

To laugh often and much.

To win the respect of intelligent people and the affection of children.

To earn the appreciation of honest critics.

To endure the betrayal of false friends.

To appreciate beauty.

To find the best in others.

To leave the world a bit better; whether by a healthy child, a garden patch, or a redeemed social condition.

To know even one life has breathed easier because you have lived. This is to have succeeded.

NO
BUNK
JUST BS
(BUSINESS SENSE)

Memoir
History, Reminiscences,
Newsletters, and Patents

Lab-Line History

To understand *No Bunk, Just BS (Business Sense)*, it will be helpful to know the history of Lab-Line, Instruments, Inc.—the laboratory instrument and equipment business that my parents, Al and Sylvia Newman, founded and is the foundation of this book.

My author's journey began as I started reading the Lab-Line monthly HI-LITER newsletters that Mary Beth Rupert, the Lab-Line Human Resource Director, gave me when my husband and I packed up my father's library at Lab-Line in 2005. The newsletters reawakened loving and lovely memories about my father, mother, and the dedicated employees, and the business they officially opened on March 5, 1952.

In 1934 my father began his business career at Precision Scientific, a family-owned laboratory instrument manufacturing company. Eventually he was promoted to executive vice president. In 1948, when the owner's sons-in-law were brought into the business, my father realized that his position was in jeopardy and he would eventually be replaced by the family members.

In 1950, my father and mother began exploring ideas and formulating a plan to start their own business to design and manufacture laboratory apparatus, instruments, and equipment. They rented office space from our neighbor, Bob Slate, who had a print shop near our home. There, my father would tinker with products and ideas after work and on the weekends.

On March 5, 1952, with physical, emotional, and financial support from family and friends (and a second mortgage on our home), LABLINE, INC, later known as Lab-Line Instruments, Inc., was born. Its first home was at 217 North Des Plaines Street in Chicago, Illinois.

I still remember scampering up and down the wide shoe-worn wooden staircase to the second-floor office in the rickety old red-brick building that was just north of the Lake Street "L" tracks and station.

Julia Amorella, my father's "Girl Friday," left her secure position at Precision Scientific and joined my parents. Julia was my father's executive secretary for 40 years, from 1934 to 1974. However, Julia didn't call him "Al" or "Mr. Newman"; her abbreviated nickname for him was just "Newman." A few original Lab-Line employees followed her example. It was their way of showing affection and appreciation for his unpretentious "No Bunk" personality.

My father and the Lab-Line engineers designed, engineered, and manufactured state-of-the-art laboratory apparatus, instruments, and equipment for research in laboratories, hospitals, universities, and government agencies. Lab-Line rapidly grew to become the largest high technology and most respected laboratory equipment company in its industry. Within 10 years Lab-Line had acquired the following subsidiaries: Chicago Surgical & Electric Co., Hudson Bay Co., Disposable Laboratory Cages, Inc., and Dynatronic Instruments Corp. In 1955, Lab-Line moved to its second home at 3070-82 West Grand Avenue in Chicago.

My father's "No Bunk" attitude, and what people now refer to as "softs skills" of communication and collaboration, were essential to the growth of the company.

My parents encouraged Lab-Line employees to make the most of their attributes and abilities and to further their education to enhance their skills.

Lab-Line also offered financial assistance to help employees to advance their education and help pay for their tuition and books. That assistance remained in place even after my father and mother had passed away.

Charitability was always practiced at Lab-Line. Donations were made to help employees, others who were in need, and/or community charities. Before the Thanksgiving Day holiday, each employee knew they would receive a turkey for their family feast. Lab-Line company picnics, anniversaries and retirement parties, and special occasions called for cakes, photos, celebrations, and an announcement or story in the *HI-LITER* newsletter.

Neither my father nor my mother boasted of their donations of money, time, and efforts, or their successful accomplishments or endeavors. My parents were unpretentious and anonymously performed "Tzedakah," which in Hebrew literally means "justice" or "righteousness" and is more commonly thought of as "charity." Their generosity included both their local and world-wide community.

They helped people by finding and purchasing the latest pharmaceutical discoveries to help their loved ones through Lab-Line connections to hospitals and university laboratories. They helped refugees find safe homes and jobs in the United States, at Lab-Line, or with companies that needed their skills. They also hosted foreign exchange students and employees and donated to centers of higher learning. When my father was building chairman of Gottlieb Hospital, they donated Lab-Line laboratory equipment for the new community hospital's laboratories.

In 1962, Lab-Line purchased property in Melrose Park, Illinois, near our home, and designed a red brick one story colonial

Williamsburg style building to meet their precise research, development, manufacturing, shipping, and office requirements.

They began building at 15th and Bloomingdale Avenues in Melrose Park and moved the company to its third and final home in September of 1963. In 1971, the two old wooden houses to south of the building were razed to make way for Lab-Line's building expansion, including new offices and a larger cafeteria for the employees.

My father had a curious mind and was man of few words. However, when he shared his words, they were direct, authentic, and meaningful; so was his personality and business approach. The words of Rabbi Joseph Tabachnik's eulogy for my father precisely describes of his personal and professional life. *"We knew Al as a gentleman, but he was often the severe critic. Al was always taken seriously because no one ever questioned his sincerity, brilliance of mind, and above all his dedication. Al demanded excellence."*

In every facet of my father's life, his principles were of the highest level. He expected no more or no less from others than he expected of himself. ***"You are making a precision instrument and someone's life depends on it—so it must be perfect."*** That statement established my father's and Lab-Line's esteemed reputation.

As a mechanical engineer who held 26 United States patents for laboratory apparatus, my father thrived on researching, designing, and manufacturing equipment to solve health problems, save people's lives, and also were used for the United States NASA (National Aeronautics and Space Administration) space research.

My father had an unusually dry sense of humor that was another facet of his reputation as a "No Bunk" task master.

As a builder, he contributed his skills and gifts to our family, his business, and to our community's synagogue, hospital, and school. Many people in our family, our community, and at Lab-Line depended on my father; he generously helped them build happier and healthier personal lives.

Several of my male friends spent their summer vacations working in the Lab-Line shipping room and on the shipping transport dock, and one of my cousins learned to efficiently operate the telephone switchboard. One of my jobs during college was delivering the latest Lab-Line catalogs to the Ohio State University biology and chemistry laboratories and to the medical center on campus.

Lab-Line employees and customers were always welcome in our home; they were emotionally and financially encouraged to better themselves by furthering their education and/or attaining a promotion.

My parents offered Lab-Line team members opportunities to purchase Lab-Line stock, as an acknowledgement of their commitment to Lab-Line's success and my parents confidence in their abilities. My father and mother demonstrated their support of people's dreams and their courage to take risks, exceed expectations, and achieve their goals. And were readily available to listen to individuals about their concerns or ideas at the plant or in our home.

Al and Sylvia Newman were dedicated to each other, their family, their community, and to every individual who helped them build Lab-Line's success. My father passed away on March 30, 1977 and my mother passed away on September 30, 2001. Their loving memories have been a blessing to my family and the copious individuals who personally knew them or knew about them through others' fond memories.

On April 29, 2005, the day after what would have been my father's 102nd birthday and 7 weeks after celebrating its 53rd anniversary, the Lab-Line doors were officially were closed.

No Bunk Lab-Line Reminiscence, Wisdom, and Inspiration

Lab-Line Life-Long Lessons

Numerous life-long lessons were learned, characters strengthened, and lives impacted through employment at Lab-Line, knowing Alexander I. and Sylvia Newman, and through the caring and compassion they shared. The following nostalgic, wise, and inspirational memoirs were generously contributed by former Lab-Line employees, family members, and friends. Some of the stories are short, others are lengthy with copious details, and every one of them was written or told to me with heartfelt sincerity. I trust you will glean wisdom, inspiration, and enjoyment from each reminiscence.

A Legacy of Loyalty and Respect - Bill Stutz

It is an honor to include Bill Stutz's as the first Lab-Line reminiscence. I will everlastingly be grateful to Bill for his kindness and thoughtfulness. If Bill had not called me, my husband and I would not have known to go to Lab-Line to collect my father's books, antique laboratory equipment, and memorabilia when the company was sold. The following is a small summary of Bill's copious Lab-Line reminiscences from 1977-2005 that thoughtfully he shared with me.

Bill was a Manufacturing Engineer, the foreman of many departments, and the Plant Manager. Before Bill worked at Lab-Line, he worked for a metal fabrication company that made products that Lab-Line purchased.

Bill met with my father in 1976 to discuss the benefits of a Wiedemann Computer Numerical Control (CNC) sheet metal punch press machine before Lab-Line invested in a new piece of equipment. When Lab-Line purchased the CNC machine it needed an expert to run their machine. Bill was that expert. He had the expertise to get the machine running to punch parts, change plans, and make programs off the prints to make new equipment.

Bill began his Lab-Line career on June 6, 1977, as the Program Director. Within 6 months, he was promoted to Foreman of the sheet metal department. Bill changed the way Lab-Line got things done to have finished products for customers with just-in-time (JIT) manufacturing that reduced the production time from 6 to 8 weeks to 4 weeks. Bill was disappointed that my father did not live to see how the CNC machine improved Lab-Line's manufacturing and production capabilities.

Below is a small collection of Bill's many detailed Lab-Line reminiscences:

The Lab-line culture was a family and a treasure. Others felt the same way I did. It was my home away from home. I would stay at work after normal hours getting the programs made and the job done.

The camaraderie is what I enjoyed from the day I started in 1977 until the day I closed the doors in 2005. I loved working with the group leaders. At one time, Lab-line included 400 people (including the outside contractors); under the roof there were 250 employees. Teamwork and trust were the foundation of Lab-Line. Everyone was equal within the large group of diverse of the employees.

I focused on being good to everyone. Like Mr. Newman, I treated people well. They respected me and my discipline to get the job done! I was the in-between guy to communicate between the plant and office.

My objective was to mix people up, including the group leaders from different departments. My plan was to make sure the diverse groups continued to get along, appreciate each other, and not turn on one another. The employees got along so well that they voted the union out. The longer I worked at Lab-Line the more attached I became to the people and the more I respected them. They respected each other and their jobs and therefore did their jobs better. I enjoyed helping some of the "old-timers" learn new jobs and how to work different pieces of equipment.

It was always a fun mixture of people when I organized a picnic Bar-B-Q; it was a treat for the whole plant. We made grills from sheet metal and 55 gallon drums. At lunch time we would grill outside in front of cafeteria. Grilling was a most effective tool for getting people together; we found many reasons to grill and celebrate. Two examples were the employees feeling good that threat of the union was over and another was meeting a sales quota. The Lab-Line baseball team also brought people together for fun and teamwork!

We also had a great relationship with the Melrose Parke Fire Department Station 2, which is located across the street from Lab-Line at 1968 N. 15th Ave.

If the fire department needed anything, we were glad to help them. When they were having trouble cooking large quantities of bacon, we were happy to make a customized bacon holder; and when they needed some boxes on the side of a new fire truck, we customized aluminum boxes for their truck.

It was a tough transition when Mr. Newman died in March 1977. I
didn't get to know him well during the 2 meetings we had, but he
did teach me to "do it yourself." I heard poignant stories from Ann
Citrone, Joe Migliore, Joe White, John Pionke, and Al Wierzbicki
—all of whom were original Lab-Line employees from 1952.

The old-timers loved Mr. Newman and were loyal to him. I learned
that everything started in the model shop. Models were often made
at night from Mr. Newman's sketches. I learned everything about
Lab-line in the model shop, including the fact that Mr. Newman
wanted things his way or it was the highway.

Mr. Newman had read a scientific study that said the color yellow
made people happy. All the manufacturing machinery in the plant
was painted yellow, even though he was color blind. I remember
traveling to Philadelphia with a Lab-Line yellow paint chip to
make sure the CNC machine was a perfect match. Even though
Mr. Newman had passed away, the Lab-Line yellow paint tradition
continued.

Mr. Newman and the engineers often solved problems after hours
at the Riviera Bowling Alley. I always felt like I took care of the
plant the way Mr. Newman took care of the office.

I drove 94 miles round-trip from my home to Lab-Line and back. I
worked from early in the morning to sometimes late at night, and I
enjoyed my job the same way every day!

I got to know Mrs. Newman when she would visit Lab-line. She
was a proud and elegant lady. She would walk through the plant, as
her husband had done, and enjoy watching the machinery running

smoothly, people operating the equipment efficiently, and the Lab-Line products being made in-house. Those were happy times in the plant because we all wanted to show off what we were doing for Mrs. Newman.

I was still doing my job with integrity, even when I thought that Lab-Line was going to be torn down. I knew everything about the Lab-Line building and had a skeleton crew working for me to pack up the equipment that had been purchased or was being auctioned off.

I decided to call Sheila, Mr. and Mrs. Newman's daughter, because I felt that someone in the family would want part of "Newman's" legacy, which included his books and antique laboratory equipment.

It would have been pitiful to have those treasures thrown out. I felt it was not right to walk out with Mr. Newman's belongings.

I stayed at the plant because I respected what Mr. Newman had done. I felt dedicated to representing him and what he had built!"

"Aunt Judie's" Dedication and Friendship –

The Amorella Family

From the *HI-LITER* newsletter December 13, 1974:

"On November 4, 1934 Julia Amorella began working for my father, the Executive Vice President of Precision Scientific. When Julia started her job, the women in the office told her she wouldn't work for him for a week.

On November 25, 1974, years later, Julia celebrated 40 years of service with Lab-Line's President, Alexander I. Newman. Mr. and Mrs. Newman presented Julia with a beautiful gold pin in a circular shape with 12 diamonds. When Mr. Newman presented the pin to Julia he explained that the circle symbolized unbroken friendship. Then, Mrs. Newman commented that Julia knew Mr. Newman long before she did.

The presentation was made in our cafeteria with all employees present. Everyone enjoyed coffee and cake in Julia's honor! Julia is planning to semi-retire the first of the year; working only two days a week."

My parents taught me to be respectful of Julia, so I always called her "Aunt Julia." When I contacted Julia's eldest nephew, Jim Amorella, I was surprised to learn that Jim and his siblings always called my "Aunt Julia" their "Aunt Judie."

My husband, Jordan, and I had the privilege and pleasure to meet and share stories about their "Aunt Judie's" nephews Jim and Dan, nieces Kathy and Dorothy, and grandnephew Billy. Her niece Jody was out of town and her nephew Jack lives in Texas.

Dan offered me a collection of beautifully handwritten quotes and detailed stories that enhanced the Amorella family's "Aunt Judie" storytelling about my father, mother, and Lab-Line.

• "The most brilliant man I ever met."

• "I learned something new every day."

• "Meticulous regarding his work, and he expected the same of others."

• "A voracious reader, and he never wasted a minute. He even read as he rode his stationary exercise bike that was in his office."

• "Could have a 'short fuse' and was known for his temper."

• "You did not want to be dressed down by Mr. Newman."

• Aunt Judie never said she worked for Mr. Newman, she always said she worked with him.

• In the early 1960's, Mr. Newman suggested that Aunt Judie sell her house and move into a brand new, beautiful apartment near Lab-Line, St. Vincent's church, and Dominick's grocery store. He even offered to help her with the rent and pay for a cab to take her back and forth to work. She asked her brother and sister-in-law what they thought. They told her to take the offer and run! Anyone who knew Mr. Newman knew he just wanted her closer to work. However, Aunt Judie declined the offer because she was concerned about what people might think.

• After Mr. Newman died, long-time clients would call just to speak to Aunt Judie on the days they knew she was working.

In fact, one long-time client specifically made appointments to see Aunt Judie when he wanted to place an order for laboratory equipment. He knew Aunt Judie would take care of him and his equipment order.

• Kathy remembered going to Lab-Line's second home on Grand Avenue on occasional Saturdays when her Aunt Judie had to finish up some work. Kathy enjoyed her task of alphabetizing Lab-Line clients' names on index cards.

• Jim remembered his Aunt Judie getting him a job working on the Lab-Line shipping docks during high school summer vacations. He remembered sitting in the back seat with his Aunt Judie, while Shifra Albert drove them and Ann Robbin to work, stopping to pick up Mr. Newman on the way to Lab-Line, in Melrose Park.

• When Aunt Judie wanted to move into the Resurrection Retirement Community, in January of 1995, she was told that she would have to wait for six months to a year because of the long waiting list. In March, Aunt Judie received a call that said an apartment was available. Everyone in the Amorella family wondered how the apartment availability happened so fast. However, they then realized it must have been that Mrs. Newman had pulled strings and donated money to make sure Aunt Judie was able to move into her apartment sooner.

(*Note from the author*: The Amorella family's generous and thoughtful sharing of photos and sweet reminiscences of their beloved "Aunt Judie" are a joyful connection to Lab-Line and my parents!)

I Loved My Job! - Lois Mosco Behrendt

Lab-Line was a family; it was a great company because all departments worked together to get a great product to our distributors. That meant all departments were a vital part in making sure the customer was happy with our service from the time the order was placed until the delivery of a well-made product.

I worked at Lab-Line for 28 years. I started in the plant manager's office coordinating the shipping orders, starting in sheet metal, machine shop, assembly, inspection, and shipping. Lab-Line always tried to promote from within, so many of us did so many other jobs (i.e., accounting moved up to computer programmer). For a short time, I worked in the engineering department, where I became familiar with drawings, bills of material, etc; and I later moved into the scheduling department, scheduling orders for production. Next I was moved up to customer service manager. This was the best job ever, I was able to hire great people and train them so they could move up to be sales reps or product managers.

Mrs. Newman was very personable and caring. She was a great support for me when my husband died very suddenly, and she offered me sage advice.

I never met Mr. Newman because he passed away before I began working at Lab-Line. I only can share what was talked about by other Lab-Line employees. Mr. Newman knew everyone like a family. One of the assembly line ladies told me that when he was in the plant he would talk to people in their native language. I thought that was very nice.

In the office, Mr. Newman knew how his employees were to do their job. If he found they were not doing things his way, he would stop and correct them.

Out of the office, Mr. Newman would join his employees at the bowling alley around the corner from the plant on Friday afternoons, after work.

I loved my job! If the business had not been sold and closed, I would still be working at Lab-Line!

An Eye-Opening Summer Job - Michael Epstein, MD

Sheila's father (A. I. Newman) was always willing to give her friends summer employment working in the Lab-Line plant in jobs that did not require technical or mechanical skills, but offered us enlightening experiences and skills. I always found Mr. Newman a bit daunting. He was always warm, but his silver-gray hair and his dapper clothes gave him an impressive and sophisticated stature.

I worked on the receiving and shipping dock for probably 8 weeks in the summer of 1962, between my junior and senior years of high school. I have a very clear recollection of the sweltering receiving and shipping dock and my co-workers. One co-worker was a young woman who must have been in her early 20's, but seemed to be very worldly and attractive to me at the time. There were also several men who did the heavy lifting. It was an eye-opener for me to talk with them as we loaded and unloaded trucks and crates.

The daily conversations were often a bit overwhelming for an inexperienced and naïve young man from River Forest (an upper-middle class suburb of Chicago). I have no idea what I was paid, but given that it was the early 1960s, I'm sure it would be a pittance compared to today's standards.

However, I learned valuable on-the-job teamwork and life-long skills working with such a diverse group of individuals that served me well throughout my career as a physician and Chief Operating Officer of Beth Israel Deaconess Medical Center in Boston, Massachusetts.

A Lesson in Humanity - Gerald M. Feldman

The most memorable and probably the most worthy life and business lesson I received was not at Lab-Line Instrument. It was on a Sunday afternoon at 1428 Clinton Place in River Forest, Illinois.

When I was 15 years old, my brother-in-law Al Newman, got me an after-school job as the "mail boy" at Precision Scientific. Via my daily mail rounds, I soon learned that Al was regarded as the operational head of the company, despite his title of Vice President. He was as tough as they came; feared and respected.

On that Sunday, my parents and I were visiting with my sister Sylvia. Meanwhile, Al was on and off the phone with what I presumed was Precision business. The phone calls went on all day and into the evening. Later that evening, the doorbell rang, and a man came in the house who I recognized as one of the factory workers. I remember how Al ushered him in. The man was very ill- at-ease, flustered, teary-eyed, and was clinging to Al's arm.

Later, I learned that Al had been calling all over the country, taking advantage of his many hospital and laboratory contacts to get special care for the man's desperately ill child. As usual, he got the job done and found medication for the child.

As important, to me at least, was the lesson in humanity I had witnessed. This tough-as-nails top executive cared enough about the "lowly" factory worker's child that he gave up his limited family time and may well have saved a child's life.

That Sunday in 1942, was a shining and unforgettable example to a 15-year-old mail boy.

In the years that followed that Sunday afternoon in 1942, I served in the United States Army during WWII.

After the war I attended Northwestern University on the G.I. Bill and graduated with a business degree. I was employed by several advertising agencies. Eventually, I originated my own advertising agency, among whose valued clients were McDonalds, Abbott Laboratories, and Lab-Line Instruments.

(*Note from the author*: When I asked my Uncle Jerry for a Lab-Line reminiscence, I was expecting an advertising agency story. Instead, I was surprised and delighted by his story, which I had never heard before.

However, the story I had heard many times before was "Jerry the Match Maker" in which my mother enjoyed recounting how one morning, my father saw my mother walking Uncle Jerry to school. He recognized that she was too young to be my uncle's mother and was determined to find out the name of the beautiful young women with red hair and great legs! I am grateful that his determination was successful!)

Job Opportunities - Linda Robbin Feldman

Lab-Line played a very important role in our lives. First and foremost was the caring spirit of Al and Sylvia Newman in offering a job to my mother, Ann Robbin, at such a vulnerable time in her life. She was 38 years old, lost her husband, and had 3 children to raise. That Al & Sylvia Newman reached out to her and offered her a job in the engineering department was indeed a blessing to Ann and her children.

While Al Newman gave Ann this wonderful opportunity to work and thus provide for her family, at the same time he enhanced the engineering department. Ann excelled at her job and was truly liked by all. She was a most diligent worker and I learned many of my skills and work ethic from her. She worked hard and did her job. She was an exemplary employee and the engineers appreciated her. Ann began working not long after her husband died, in 1955. She retired in 1980 and moved to Arizona.

Ann had many good friends from Lab-Line, one of which was Shifra Albert. Shifra always passed on her "stock market tips," which allowed my mother to purchase a myriad of small shares over the years. After Ann passed, it was left to me to dispose of all those stocks. It kept me very busy, but Ann loved those little checks that came every month. (Thank you, Shifra!)

Al Newman had a genuine, sort-of half smile, and a heart of gold. He was an amazing man.

I had the good fortune to have my first summer job at Lab-Line when I was 16 years old.

Thank you, Al Newman, for allowing me to work there too.

Running the switchboard (yes, switchboard) was quite an experience.

Answering the phone in a professional manner and then connecting the callers to whomever they wanted to speak with was a challenge—crossing wires, connecting the wires, etc., is something I will never forget. I also learned to collate and stuff envelopes and to this day I am the fastest person in my office!

Planning for Success - Bruce M. Morical

I learned many lessons about being successful during the 34 years I was a Lab-Line employee. The two most significant lessons were planning on a monthly, weekly, and daily basis and being prepared for sales calls. Both Mr. and Mrs. Newman always emphasized the importance of planning. Clear and prompt sales reports and product knowledge were Lab-Line business standards. I think the most important factors in Lab-Line's success were honesty with our customers, the steadfast management, the dedicated people, and great marketable products.

My Lab-Line memories began on March 2, 1962. I was looking for an outside sales position. I applied to Lab-Line at 3050 W. Grand Ave in Chicago, which was their second business location. First, I was introduced to Julia Amorella, Mr. Newman's secretary, who shared the office with Mr. Newman. Then I interviewed with Mr. Newman. Evidently the interview went well enough that I was introduced to the sales staff and taken on a tour through the whole building, manufacturing and all. Later that morning, I left with a new job!

A significant memory was being introduced to the product line to familiarize myself with it, so I could attend trade shows and conferences. I remember that Mr. Newman had just introduced the Alumaloy clamp line. In demonstrating the two clamp lines at a trade show, the competitor's clamp that was made of Zinc melted at a much lower temperature and was hazardous in a laboratory situation. The new Alumaloy clamp passed the safety test and did not melt.

I always experienced additional training for new products during my sales territory assignments. My first assigned sales territory was Houston, Texas.

128

The territory comprised the states of Texas, Louisiana, Arkansas, and Oklahoma. For the next 3 years, I worked with NASA, the universities of these states, and our dealers. I transferred back to the Chicago area and worked 4 more years covering the states of Illinois, Iowa, Wisconsin, Minnesota, Michigan, and Ohio.

Then Mr. Newman asked if I would cover the Washington, DC territory, which included Pennsylvania, Delaware, New Jersey, Maryland, North Carolina, and Virginia. I was assigned to call on our dealers, universities, and pharmaceutical companies. My family and I enjoyed a good life in DC, and I remember Mr. and Mrs. Newman coming to our home and meeting my family. While working in DC, we received the largest order we ever had from the National Institutes of Health. It was for 33 walk-in incubators and cold rooms. It was a very exciting achievement for me and Lab-Line.

Before Mr. Newman passed away in 1977, he offered me the opportunity to invest in Lab-Line stock. I felt fortunate to accept his offer.

Mr. and Mrs. Newman always offered me generous hospitality in their home. I will never forget Mrs. Newman elegantly dressed and grilling steaks in their family room fireplace. Mr. Newman had the grill designed and manufactured at Lab-Line.

I saw Mrs. Newman for the last time before she passed in 2001. She had invited me up to her apartment for soup and a sandwich at their Water Tower condominium. I was pleased to see the lovely color pen and ink drawing of Mr. and Mrs. Newman's home in River Forest, which my wife Cindy and I had commissioned for them in 1976.

Learning Opportunity & Skills = Success -
Mary Beth Rupert

I worked for Lab-Line from 1986–2005. My 19-year career at Lab-Line started as an accounts payable clerk and I also calculated the payroll for the factory workers. After 6 months, I asked if I could start night school to take a business class. My request was approved. Lab-Line had a wonderful tuition reimbursement policy which I took advantage of. If I received an A, tuition and books were paid 100%, which was a wonderful incentive to get straight A's!

A few years later, I was promoted to the Purchasing Department as an Expeditor and continued going to school to get my Associates Degree. From Purchasing I was promoted to the Credit Manager where I had 4 employees reporting to me. I finished my Associates Degree and enrolled at Elmhurst College to obtain my Bachelor of Science degree!

After several years of running Accounts Receivable I was promoted to be a Cost Accountant, another wonderful and challenging opportunity to learn new skills and develop myself. A couples years later, the Director of Human Resources was retiring and I was graduating from college and was asked to take over HR and went back to school to learn new skills and not only become OSHA certified, but tool\k my boards to receive my HR certification.

I was able to learn more about the company by working a day in each department of the factory. It was a rewarding learning experience. I pulled material for orders, built a shaker from start to finish in one day, bent sheet metal, filed down sheet metal parts to make them smooth and worked in the shipping department.

Lab-Line was located across the street from Melrose Park's Fire Department Station 2. We had a very good relationship with the fire fighters.

When they needed some sheet metal work done for their trucks, Bill Stutz would oversee the work to make sure it met their needs. Days when we had luncheons for the employees, we shared the left-overs with the fire fighters, which they loved and appreciated.

The night before the United States became involved in the war against Iraq, Lab-Line received an order for $150,000 worth of incubators. At that time, the government could not place an order for more than $100,000 unless there was a state of war. When that order came in we knew something was imminent. The next day, we learned about Dessert Storm. The incubators were to be used in the sand for testing to see what our troops/soldiers were being exposed to.

Today, there are very few many companies with the Lab-Line tradition of treating employees well and believing in them. I've been in HR ever since I worked at Lab-Line. The reason why I am as successful as I am today is because of the learning opportunities I was given while working at Lab-Line.

(*Note from the author:* Mary Beth is a skilled HR Director and thoughtful woman. Because of Mary Beth's kindness my collection of Lab-Line *HI-LITER* newsletters were saved from being discarded and thrown in a dumpster. I am most grateful to Mary Beth's kindhearted gift of Lab-Line *HI-LITER* newsletters, which became a family treasure and foundation for this book.)

Do the Right Thing - Michael A. Sobel, CPCU

As a family and business friend, the following are my thoughts and lessons from the past that I learned from Al and Sylvia Newman.

• Listen, be professional, and always do the right thing whether it benefits you or not. This ALWAYS works, in the long run.

• Help others if you can, and Al and Sylvia did!

• Take care of your crew first, and Al and Sylvia did!

• The crew then took care of them by making great products! (I remember some of those great crew members.)

Al and Sylvia were tough on me, but always respectful.

I do miss them. I still have fond memories of both of them!

Similarities and Synchronicity - Ali N. Syed, PhD

I was not eager to tour the red-brick, ivy-covered one-story building at 15th and Bloomingdale in Melrose Park, Illinois when I was searching for a new site for my business, Avlon Industries. The Colonial Williamsburg architecture was not my style. I hesitated to take the time to go inside the building. However, I changed my mind and was glad I did. When I walked through the building and saw the front offices, laboratories, cafeteria, and the manufacturing and shipping areas. I knew the building was perfectly designed for my business, as it was for Lab-Line.

(*Note from the author:* Dr. Ali N. Syed is the president of Avlon Industries who purchased the Lab-Line building in October of 2005 and moved into the building in March of 2006. I am thrilled that the Lab-Line building, which my parents designed and built, was not destroyed. Instead of being torn down as planned, the building was sold to Avlon Industries and is now the home of another family-owned international manufacturing business.

The owner, Ali N. Syed—who is a master chemist and has a PhD in business management, told me how much he appreciates how well my parents designed and constructed the building. He has only modified the original layout of the building by adding a conference room near the cafeteria and another office space that used to be a laboratory. The plant area that was originally designed for manufacturing laboratory equipment was re-designed to warehouse incoming raw and chemical materials to create the widely-used and efficacious professional hair care products Avlon sells worldwide.

I am delighted by the similarities between Avlon Industries and Lab-Line.

Dr. Syed uses my father's executive office as his office and my father's library continues to be used as a library and conference room.

Dr. Syed's wife and children also work for Avlon Industries. As Executive Assistant Marissa Gutierrez told me, *"We are a family!"*

Dr. Syed has been granted 28 patents and my father was granted 26 patents. The Avlon goal is *"to provide the very best products that advanced research and innovative thinking can offer, and always with an eye toward advancing hair technology."* The objective of Lab-Line was "to provide the scientists with the best-made, best-performing, and most modern instruments to do their work…" Avlon Industries, as Lab-Line had been, is generous and charitable to individuals and organizations.

In September of 2008, my husband, our elder son, and I were eagerly waiting for our younger son, daughter-in-law, and two-year old granddaughter to arrive at O'Hare International Airport from Saõ Paulo, Brazil.

When people began exiting the customs area, I approached an attractive and friendly looking couple and asked if they were on the plane from Saõ Paulo. They asked who I was waiting, and I told them. Coincidentally, they were sitting near Noah, Kelly and Yasmin and told me how much they enjoyed our family, especially Yasmin. Then we said good-bye.

A few months later, I Bill Stutz let me know that the Lab-Line building had not been torn down, but instead was sold. I was relieved and curious to know about the company that purchased the building.

I called the Melrose Park Chamber of Commerce to find out who had saved the Lab-Line building. I learned that Avlon Industries was the new owner. I immediately searched the internet to learn more about Avlon Industries. When I clicked on the About Page, I saw the photo of the president of Avlon Industries, Dr. Ali N. Syed.

I immediate called Dr. Syed. I re-introduced myself as Sheila Neman Glazov, the daughter of the original owners of the building; and reminded him that we had met at the airport a few months earlier when we were waiting for Yasmin and her parents to arrive from Saõ Paulo. Of course, Dr. Syed was astonished by another family coincidence. We had a lovely conversation, and I told him I would stay in touch with him about the book I was planning about Lab-Line.

I am honored to share Dr. Syed's story. The similarities and synchronicity between Dr. Syed and Lab-Line is another remarkable connection to my family.)

Saving the Love of His Life! - Sheila Newman Glazov

In December 1960, only a few weeks after my parents had returned from their first business trip to Europe and the United Kingdom, I recall walking into our family room and seeing my parents sitting on the couch together. My father's arm was gently wrapped around my mother's right shoulder. My mother sat quietly with tears in her eyes, I was sure she was going to tell me something horrific about my father's heart condition.

"Daddy, are you OK?" I asked.

"I am OK," he said. "It is your mother who is sick and going to the hospital for tests."

My thoughts and emotions swirled as I attempted to process what my father had just said. How could my mother be so sick that she was crying?

Those tests were performed with Lab-Line equipment, which my father donated to all the labs at Gottlieb Hospital near our home, and confirmed that my mother had tuberculosis (TB). The doctors believed she had contracted it during her recent travels overseas.

In 1960, the Lab-Line business network had grown to include the University of Chicago. Through my parents' business relationship, my father was able to have my mother admitted to a special TB section of the hospital where the TB research was being conducting.

On the Monday morning after the winter holiday school vacation, I started the week at Oak Park River Forest High School, and my mother started her 6-month residence at Albert Merritt Billings

Hospital, which a the time was one of four hospitals that formed the University of Chicago Clinics.

I distinctly recall my mother telling me that my father *refused* to have her admitted to a TB sanitarium.

At that time, Lab-Line was only 8-years-old and my father depended on my mother, his life partner and business partner, for day-to-day and critical decisions. Most mornings, my father drove almost an hour from our home to check on my mother and discuss Lab-Line business with her, speak with her doctors, and then drive 30 minutes to Lab-Line. Depending on my father's schedule, he would leave work early to drive back to the hospital to see my mother and afterwards drive home to have dinner with me.

Each Saturday and Sunday, my father and I would spend most of the day visiting with my mother and discussing Lab-Line business. Before we went into my mother's room we were required to put a white hospital gown over our clothes and wear a white facial mask, because TB is highly contagious. When we left her room, we had to deposit our masks and gowns in a special waste basket outside her room and thoroughly wash our hands.

On Sunday evenings, we routinely dined at the Tropical Hut, which was a famous Hyde Park, South Side of Chicago restaurant. After dinner, my father and I would deliver take-out dinners from the "Hut" to my mother and nurses on the TB floor and say good-night to my mother.

One of the many responsibilities I took over from my mother was packing my father's suitcase for Lab-Line business trips. My mother had precisely instructed me to carefully pack my father's tie, shirt, pocket handkerchief, socks, and shoes together with the appropriate color suit. No errors could be made. My father was color blind and could not coordinate his attire. She was afraid he would embarrass himself.

During my mother's stay at the hospital, I celebrated my 16th birthday. Family and friends organized lovely planned and surprise celebrations and gifts. Nevertheless, when people asked me what wanted for my birthday, my answer was always: *"I want my mother to come home cured! I want to kiss my mother!"*

After 5 months of trial and error with a new TB medication, including one dosage that paralyzed my mother, the doctors and my parents determined that the medication was not working. The only option to cure my mother's TB was a 10-hour experimental surgical procedure. Before her operation, the doctors allowed my mother to come home for a few days. I remember how joyfully normal life felt knowing my mother was at home. However, I was jolted back into reality on the first morning I was leaving for school.

"Love you. See you later." I said before naturally leaning forward to give her a hug and a kiss good-bye.

"Sheila, remember I cannot kiss you." she reminded me.

We both began to cry. I bolted out the front door, running and weeping all the way to meet my friend Alice Kaufman to catch the school bus.

The walk to and from the bus stop and the bus ride to school was not the same as it had been before my mother's TB diagnosis. Alice and I usually walked and sat on the bus by ourselves. There were students who did not want to be near me because, either they had heard about my mother having TB and/or their parents had told them the news, and they were afraid to come in contact with me. I was grateful that Alice and a few other close friends, their parents, and our neighbors were properly informed and knew I was not contagious.

The morning my mother underwent the 10-hour experimental surgery to remove the diseased upper lobe of her right lung, my father, my Aunt Charlotte (my mother's younger sister), and I anxiously waited in the hospital's surgical lounge.

The doctors had previously informed us that one team would be cutting under my mother's right breast, around her side, and up her shoulder blade to remove the upper lobe of her right lung. Another team would remove the TB-diseased lobe. Finally, another team would close the extensive incision.

I can still visualize myself sitting between my father and my aunt and listening to the different doctors' periodic surgical reports. We all were elated when the last surgeon reported that my mother had survived the surgery and the procedure was successful.

My mother was a healthy and determined 44-year-old woman who recuperated so quickly that she returned home in 2 weeks, instead of the normal 4 to 6 week recuperation period. My father had my Uncle Sydney and Aunt Helen, who owned an interior design company, beautifully redecorated my parents' bedroom for my mother's homecoming and recuperation.

My mother made a complete recovery. She became an active member of the Chicago Lung Association, practiced a consistent respiratory therapy regime, and was careful about environmental changes and challenges to her ability to breathe properly.

My beloved mother lived to be 84-years-of-age and was able to enjoy her life that was abundantly filled with loving blessings from her family, friends, and Lab-Line.

Writing the *NO BUNK* chapters and editing others' Lab-Line memoirs reinforced my treasured knowledge about my father's and mother's generosity to help others in need of medical assistance with their Lab-Line equipment and business network of doctors, researchers, health care facilities, and medications.

When I think about all the previous Lab-Line reminiscences, the most momentous and life-changing was my father's Lab-Line connection to the University of Chicago. **It was the connection that saved my mother's life and the love of my father's life!**

Lab-Line Newsletters

LAB-LINE HI-LITER

Vol. I, Issue 1   January 16, 1970

"HI-LITER" GOES TO PRESS

The management of Lab-Line is pleased to announce the beginning of a newspaper for and by the Lab-Line employees. It is our hope that this newspaper will bring about a new awareness for each of us in regards to the Company, our fellow employees and our departments.

Over the years, Lab-Line has grown very rapidly, to the point where we now have almost two hundred members in our employee family. Some have been with us since our first year in business; others have just recently joined us. It takes time to get to know everyone, and it is our hope that an employee newsletter of this type will help us to become friends much faster, or to renew old friendships.

The LAB-LINE HI-LITER will be published every two weeks for distribution with the paychecks. A portion of the paper will be devoted to such items as safety, housekeeping, Company policies, and philosophy. The rest of the paper will be devoted to YOU. We want to know what you are doing, who had a baby, who got married or engaged, who is sick, (no one, we hope), who is having an anniversary with the Company, who just joined the Lab-Line family, and so forth.

In order for us to get all of this information, we have asked some of you to act as our official reporters. The reporters are:

Office:	Kay Smith
Engineering:	Newton Reed
Plant:	J.P. McSwain
	Alice Brown

If any of you have any news for our newspaper, please give it to one of our talented reporters or bring it on a piece of paper to Personnel.

Let's all pitch in to make the HI-LITER a big success.

DON'T QUIT

When things go wrong as they some-
   times will,
When the road you're trudging seems
   all up hill,
When the funds are low and the debts
   are high,
And you want to smile, but you have
   to sigh,
When care is pressing you down a bit,
Rest if you must, but don't you quit.
Life is queer with its twists and
   turns,
As everyone of us sometimes learns,
And many a failure turns about
When he might have won had he stuck
   it out;
Don't give up though the pace seems
   slow,
You may succeed with another blow.
Success is failure turned inside out-
The silver tint of the clouds of
   doubt,
And you never can tell how close you
   are,
It may be near when it seems so far;
So stick to the fight when you're
   hardest hit-
It's when things seem worst that you
   must not quit.

                Author Unknown

KAY'S COMMENTS
        Kay Smith, Reporter

If there is ANYONE who hasn't heard, KAREN WOODFORD will be married May 2nd Best wishes to STEVE and KAREN....ED JEPSON, Ad Manager, is writing a manual on Fords...seems ED has had so many different problems with his car, he feels he is an expert on the care and feeding of Fords...The first half of our Bowling season is over with Val Sobieski, Roger Yates, and John Pionke in 1st place. In 2nd place are Bev Glinka, Al Larson, and Dave Pooler ...But for the real games, stay after. SHIFRA ALBERT is celebrating a birthday the 23rd...ED ASTRIN and his wife, Phyllis are celebrating their 40th Wedding Anniversary.

HI-LITER

LAB-LINE

VOL. 3   ISSUE 14   **JULY 12, 1974**

THE OBJECTIVES OF LAB-LINE SHALL BE TO PROVIDE THE SCIENTIST WITH THE BEST-MADE, BEST-PERFORMING, AND MOST MODERN INSTRUMENTS TO DO HIS WORK; TO PROVIDE JOBS AND JOB SECURITY FOR THOSE WHO APPLY THEMSELVES CONSISTENTLY AND EFFECTIVELY TO THEIR JOBS; AND TO MAKE A PROFIT TO CONTINUE ITS OPERATIONS AND MAINTAIN ITS OBJECTIVES.

WELCOME BACK VACATIONERS!

FREE COFFEE!!!   FREE COFFEE!!!

All Lab-Line employees' birthdays for the week, will be celebrated every Monday, morning til night, with free coffee.

Come early on Monday and join your friends in the celebration!

As you know, for those who do not care for coffee, you may select hot chocolate, hot tea or chicken soup.

We have heard many comments since we started our free coffee, Monday, July 1st. Good, bad or indifferent, here are just a few.....
"Wonderful! Thanks a million!"
"Great! It tastes better than when I pay for it!"
"Any objections if I have a couple at lunch?"
"I think it is nice!"
"How about free coffee all week?"
"Ugh! I hate coffee! I'd rather have the 15¢.

VISITORS AT LAB-LINE

We were fortunate to have distinguished visitors at Lab-Line this past week. Mr. Fred Pfaehler, Adolf Kuhner AG, Basel, Switzerland and his charming wife, were our guests on June 27th & June 28th.

TWINKLE TWINKLE SUPERSTAR
TO THOSE WHO SAID YOU'D NOT GO FAR,
YOU SHOWED THEM GUTS, YOU SHOWED THEM NERVE
NOW! SHOW THEM THE LAB-LINE VERVE!

100.7% SHIPPING QUOTA --- JUNE 1974

We did it! We blew the lid off for the month of June and reached 100.7% of our Shipping Quota!

A free chicken dinner is in store for all Lab-Line employees. Date to be announced!

IN MEMORIUM

Mr. Ben Preiser, founder of Preiser Scientific Company of Charleston, West Virginia, Passed away on Saturday, June 21st.

Ben started his company in 1924 and this was the 50th Anniversary of the company.

Ben chose Charleston, West Virginia, because it was in the heart of heavy chemical industry and coal mining and Preiser Scientific became an important distributor in the Scientific Instrument field and was one of Lab-Line's first and valuable customers.

In recent years, Ben was taking things easier as his son, Alvin, became more involved in the management of the company.

A good husband and father, he will be missed by all his relatives and friends. Our deepest sympathy to his wife, Kate, and the entire Preiser family. His memory will always be a constant inspiration to all who knew him.

"THE LIFE YOU SAVE WITH LAB-LINE INSTRUMENTS, MAY BE YOUR OWN. BUILD THEM BETTER."

HI-LITER

LAB-LINE

VOL. 4   ISSUE 12   OCTOBER 1975

THE OBJECTIVES OF LAB-LINE SHALL BE TO PROVIDE THE SCIENTIST AND OUR DEALERS WITH
THE BEST-MADE, BEST PERFORMING, AND MOST MODERN INSTRUMENTS AT COMPETITIVE PRICES;
TO PROVIDE JOBS AND JOB SECURITY FOR THOSE OF OUR EMPLOYEES WHO APPLY THEMSELVES
CONSISTENTLY AND EFFECTIVELY TO THEIR JOBS; AND TO MAKE A REASONABLE PROFIT TO
CONTINUE ITS OPERATIONS AND MAINTAIN ITS OBJECTIVES. IF WE MAINTAIN THESE OBJECTIVES,
NO POTENTIAL USER CAN POSSIBLY REFUSE TO BUY OUR INSTRUMENTS.

We Proudly Salute

In recognition of the many years of
service and devotion, Lab-Line Instruments acknowledges its appreciation of
the following employees whose anniversary is celebrated in OCTOBER with two
or more years of service:

Al Wierzbicki	15 years
Al Leach	14 years
Lowell Lathrop	12 years
Booker Bell	9 years
Al Jackson	8 years
Kaye Smith	7 years
Pat Bryant	3 years
Larry Poland	3 years
Faye Vojtech	3 years
Gene King	2 years
Tony Loquercio	2 years

HAPPY BIRTHDAY to:

Carlos Mendoza	Oct. 1st
Al Kaatz	Oct. 2nd
Jackie Pearson	Oct. 4th
Denise Adamson	Oct. 11th
Geraldine Burke	Oct. 21st

Happy Anniversary

To Mr. & Mrs. Alexander I. Newman,
best wishes from all of us at Lab-Line
as you celebrate your Thirty-Sixth
Wedding Anniversary on October 22nd.

THINK AHEAD

WHAT IS 1 PART PER MILLION?

One part per million is equal to:

- One inch in 16 miles;
- One minute in two years;
- A one gram needle in a ton of hay;
- One penny in $10,000;
- One ounce of salt in 62,500 pounds
- One large mouthful of food when
  compared with the food a person
  will eat in a lifetime.
- One drop of Vermouth in 80 "fifths" -
  a very dry martini!

SOMEONE HAS TO MAKE IT HAPPEN
AND THAT SOMEONE IS

YOU!

MAKE LAB-LINE THE "THINK AHEAD" COMPANY

LAB-LINE HI-LITER

VOL. 4   ISSUE 6   MAY 9, 1975

THE OBJECTIVES OF LAB-LINE SHALL BE TO PROVIDE THE SCIENTIST WITH THE BEST-MADE, BEST-PERFORMING, AND MOST MODERN INSTRUMENTS AT COMPETITIVE PRICES TO DO HIS WORK; TO PROVIDE JOBS AND JOB SECURITY FOR THOSE WHO APPLY THEMSELVES CONSISTENTLY AND EFFECTIVELY TO THEIR JOBS; AND TO MAKE A PROFIT TO CONTINUE ITS OPERATIONS AND MAINTAIN ITS OBJECTIVES. IF WE MAINTAIN THESE OBJECTIVES, NO POTENTIAL CUSTOMER CAN POSSIBLY REFUSE TO BUY OUR INSTRUMENTS.

HAPPY BIRTHDAY to..

John Dodge	May 24
Carmen Ramos	May 5
Mike Barsanti	May 8
Vic Milas	May 8
Sylvia Newman	May 10
Ismael Caceres	May 16
John Iacobellis	May 28
Noah Jeremish Glazov	May 26

****

We Proudly Salute

In recognition of the many years of service and devotion, Lab-Line Instruments acknowledges its appreciation of the following employees whose anniversary is celebrated in MAY with two or more years of service:

Julia Amorella	23 years
Ted Novak	19 years
Mike Ciebien	18 years
Antonio Bergamini	5 years
Henry Erbach	3 years
Tim Geminn	3 years
Ann Karbach	2 years

****

DO IT TODAY!

TOMORROW MAY BE TOO LATE!

****

LOVE ME ALWAYS

You say you love me but sometimes you don't show it. In the beginning, you couldn't do enough for me. Now you seem to take me for granted... some days I even wonder if I mean anything at all to you.

Maybe when I'm gone, you'll appreciate me and all the things I do for you. I'm responsible for getting the food on your table, for your clean shirt, for the welfare of your children... a thousand and one things you want and need. Why, if it weren't for me you wouldn't even have a car. I've kept quiet and waited to see how long it would take for you to realize how much you really need me.

Cherish me...take care of me and I'll continue to take good care of you.

WHO AM I? I AM YOUR JOB.

(Contributed by Vera Hartke)
****
THOUGHTS

Trouble is often opportunity knocking.

Small cars are great. You can squeeze twice as many into a traffic jam.

If you tell a man that there are 300 billion stars in the universe, he'll believe you, but if you tell him a bench has just been painted, he has to touch it to be sure.

Cooperation is doing with a smile what you have to do anyway.
****
LET'S ALL MAKE LAB-LINE THE "THINK AHEAD" COMPANY

FROM THE CULINARY CORNER........
........ANN ROBBIN

QUICK FRUIT COBBLER

1/4 cup flour
2 eggs
1/3 cup milk
1/3 teaspoon salt
2 tablespoons sour cream or yogurt
Grated lemon rind or 2 tablespoons
liqueur of your choice

2 teaspoons butter or oil
2-1/2 to 3 cups cut-up fruit

Put the flour,eggs, milk, salt, sour cream,
or liqueur in the blender container and
whirl 1 minute on high speed.

Butter the pan or mold (any heatproof pan
will do - even a 9 inch fry pan)and place
over medium heat. Pour one quarter of
batter in the pan and spread it over the
whole bottom of pan and cook it quickly
like a pancake. Remove from heat. Put
the fruit on top of the cake and spread
it well, then pour the remainder of
batter on top. Bake in a preheated 375°
oven for 35 to 40 minutes.

Following combinations of fruit and liqueur
may be used:

Pears and rum (or ground cloves)
Apples and Applejack (or cinnamon)
Bananas and rum
Cherries and cherry brandy or kirsch
Strawberries and kirsch or Curacao
Peaches and bourbon or brandy
Apricots with kirsch, cognac or brandy
Blueberries with lime rind and bourbon
Italian plums and lemon rind.
****

VIRGINIA'S VESTPOCKET VIEWS..........

Congratulations to John and Hazel
Wilkinson! They became citizens of the
USA on Tuesday, September 23rd. We are
still waiting for your recipe of York-
shire Pudding, John! In exchange, we
will give you some good ole USA recipes
for tacos, egg roll, bagels, lasagna,
kielbasa, etc. etc. etc. etc.

The worst kind of reducing pill is the
one who keeps telling you how she did it!

Joanne Gorman's son, Jeff, thinks his
mom is getting good at driving. She
just learned to paralyze park!

An ounce of soap will make 1,562,500
bubbles!

Our mechanical minded Kaye Smith complain-
ed to the telephone company that the
extension cord on her phone was too
long. She asked the Service Department
to "Just pull it in at your end until
I tell you to stop".

Remember when charity was a virtue
instead of a deduction?

John Migut does have his problems. First
with his garage door and now locking his
keys in his car. Ho-hum! What else is
new, John?

Did you know that it takes 72 different
muscles to speak one word?

Ann Robbin was going to give us a recipe
on how to bake a 2-1/2 to 3 inch sirloin
steak but changed her mind...wonder why?

Kitchen Hint: Recipes that specify
"sprinkle with lemon juice" were a bit
of a problem until I found that a small,
glass salt shaker provided an excellent
way to sprinkle small quantities of
lemon juice.

Blanche James says: "An exclamation point
is a period that has blown its top!"

Linda Nelson, Sunday School Teacher,
was trying to instill in her young class
the joys of shouting "Hallelujah!"
She asked, "What word do church members
shout with great joy?"
One youngster answered "Bingo!"
****

MAKE LAB-LINE THE "THINK AHEAD" COMPANY

The United States Patents of Alexander I. Newman

My father was granted 26 United States Patents for his inventions. Below are 22 United States Patents for laboratory equipment and instruments that were granted to Alexander I. Newman over a 31-year period between 1936 until 1967. Unfortunately, I was unable to locate the other 4 patents that he was granted.

1. Motor-Driven Color Screen—granted December 15, 1936
2. Variable Pressure Apparatus—granted November 29, 1938
3. Combined Digesting and Distilling Apparatus—granted October 31, 1939
4. Water Still—granted November 21, 1939
5. Water Bath—granted November 21, 1939
6. Titration Testing Apparatus—granted June 11, 1940
7. Fume Tube—granted August 6, 1940
8. Titration Apparatus Illuminator—granted October 1, 1940
9. Distillation Testing Apparatus—granted November 19, 1940
10. Crude Fiber Digestion Apparatus—granted November 19, 1940
11. Electric Timer—granted February 5, 1941
12. Electric Timer—granted April 29, 1941
13. Still—granted September 2, 1941
14. United Titration Apparatus—granted December 22, 1942
15. Gas-Analyzing Apparatus—granted August 21, 1945
16. Flask Heater—granted October 12, 1948
17. Specimen Holder—granted April 5, 1949

18. Distillation Testing Apparatus—granted August 15, 1950

19. Combined Electric Heater and Magnetic Stirrer—granted February 7, 1967

20. Magnetic Stirring Bar—granted February 13, 1973

21. Multi-Block-Type Test Tube Heater—granted November 6, 1973

22. Incubator-Shaker—granted September 10, 1974

Examples of the United States Patents
of Alexander I. Newman

Variable Pressure Apparatus—granted November 29, 1938

Nov. 29, 1938. A. I. NEWMAN 2,138,527

VARIABLE PRESSURE APPARATUS
Filed June 6, 1935

2 Sheets—Sheet 2

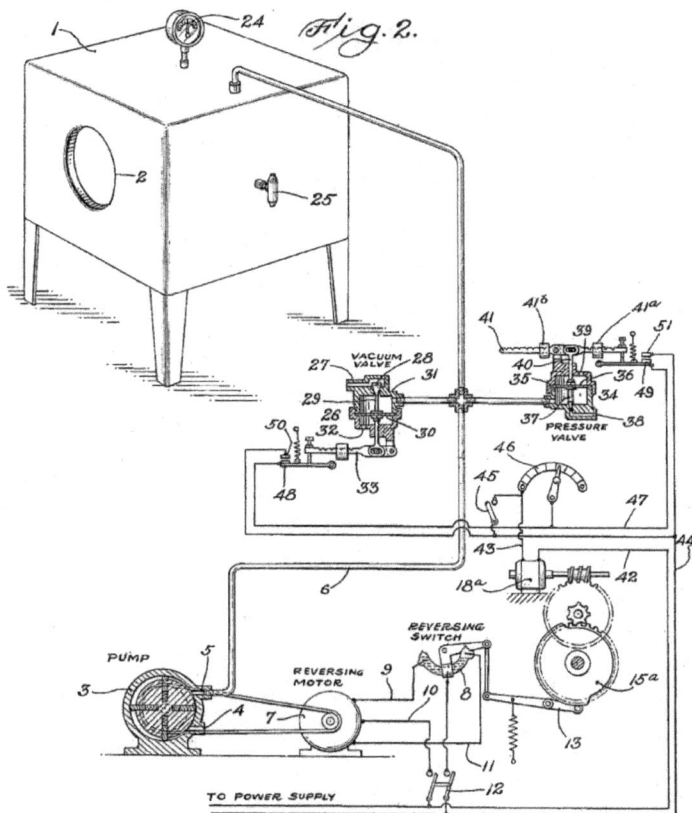

Fig. 2.

Inventor;
Alexander I. Newman
BY
Parker Carleon Pitzer Hubbard
Attorney's.

148

Combined Digesting and Distilling Apparatus—granted October 31, 1939

Oct. 31, 1939.   A. I. NEWMAN   Des. 117,406

COMBINED DIGESTING AND DISTILLING APPARATUS

Filed July 20, 1939

Fig.1.

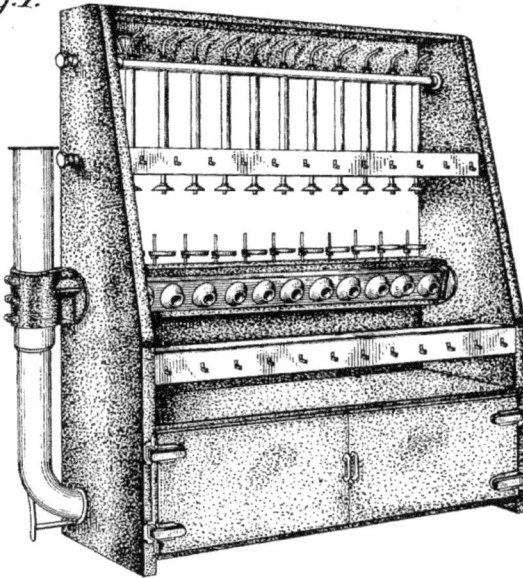

Fig.2.

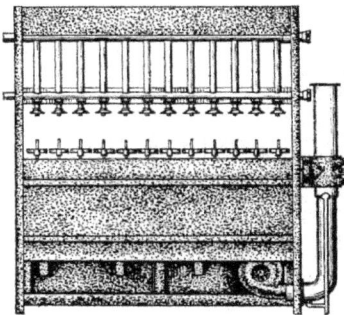

Inventor
Alexander I. Newman
BY
Parker, Carlton, Pitzman & Hubbard.

Attorneys.

Motor-Driven Color Screen—granted
December 15, 1936, Figure #1

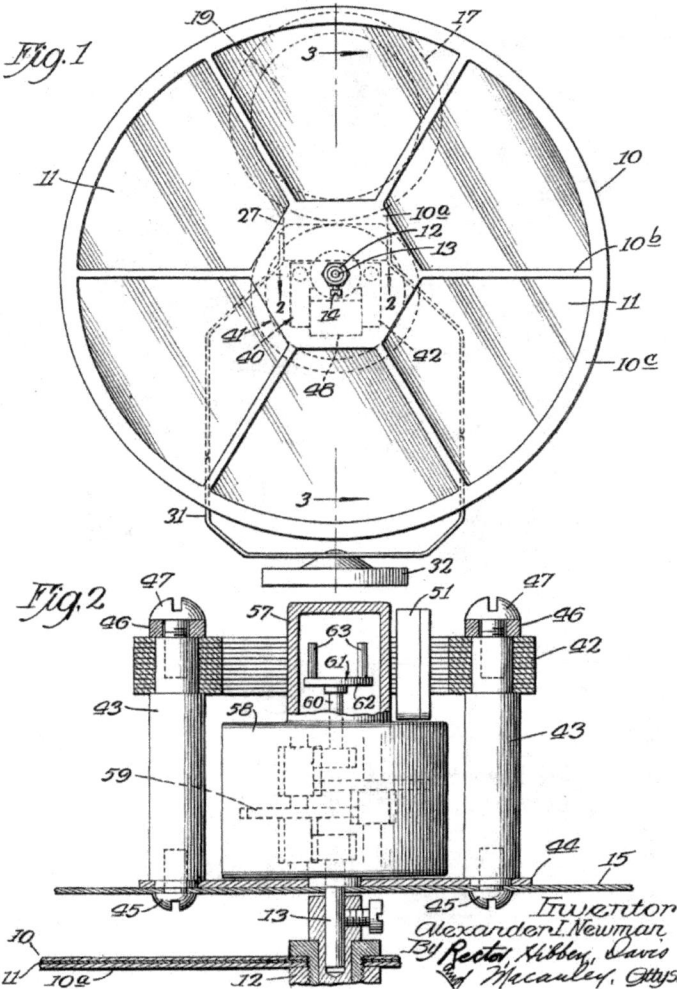

Dec. 15, 1936.　　　A. I. NEWMAN　　　2,064,625

MOTOR DRIVEN COLOR SCREEN

Filed Sept. 8, 1933　　　2 Sheets–Sheet 1

Motor-Driven Color Screen—granted
December 15, 1936, Figure #3

Dec. 15, 1936.   A. I. NEWMAN   2,064,625

MOTOR DRIVEN COLOR SCREEN

Filed Sept. 8, 1933   2 Sheets—Sheet 2

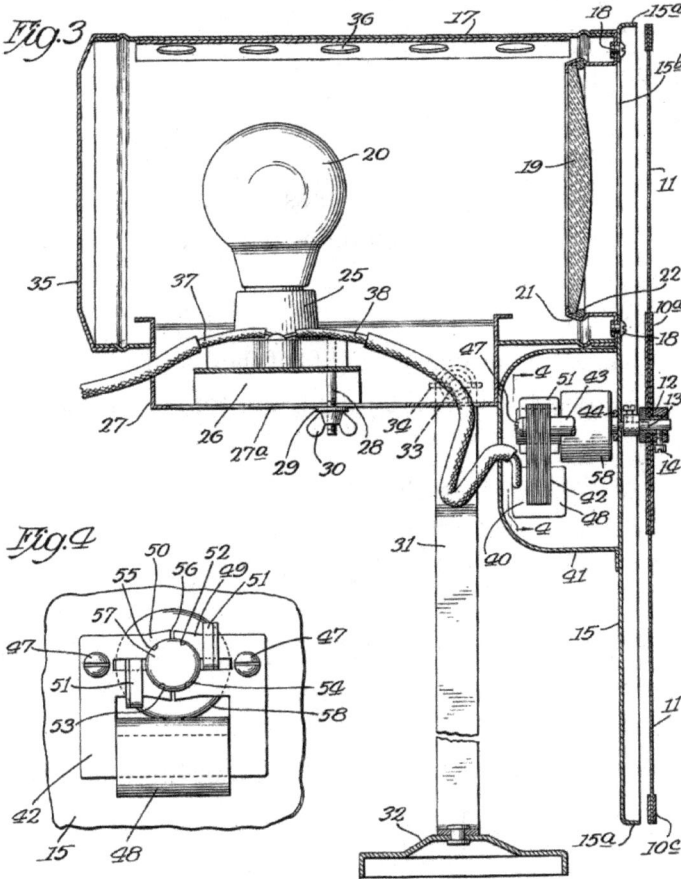

Fig.3

Fig.4

Inventor:
Alexander I. Newman
By Rector, Hibben, Davis & Macauley, Attys.

Acknowledgements

It is a privilege and a pleasure to acknowledge the following individuals who graciously and generously shared their reminiscences about Lab-Line and my parents, read my manuscript, and offered me advice, and support throughout my writing process.

This book has been an adventure of discoveries and a labor of love because of each individual and their contributions!

Bill Stutz, if not for your thoughtfulness to call me to let me know about my father's books and belongings, *No Bunk, Just BS* would not have been written.

Mary Beth Rupert, your generous gift of the Lab-Line *HI-LITER* newsletters helped to create the foundation for *No Bunk, Just BS.*

Amorella Family Members (Jim, Dorothy, Kathy, Dan, and Billy), I loved sharing our heartfelt stories of your "Aunt Judie" and my "Aunt Julia." I am most grateful for your thoughtfulness.

Lois Mosco Behrendt, I am thrilled I found you and added your Lab-Line "family" stories to *No Bunk*!

Michael Epstein, your story is now part of our life-long friendship and sweet childhood memories.

Gerald M. Feldman (Uncle Jerry), your reminiscence was a profound surprise! "Shmeilek," thank you for your remarkable story, for being my parents' "Match Maker," and for being a peer reader of my manuscript!

Linda Robbin Feldman (Cousin Linda), what a delight to reconnect through your story and your mother's. Now we have added to our sweet family memories!

Bruce M. Morical, I am delighted that I was able to find you through your son Greg's LinkedIn profile. I am honored that your memories of my parents and Lab-Line are part of *No Bunk*!

Michael A. Sobel, you were the first person to send me your wonderful reminiscences of my parents for my book. Now we both have added more memories to life-time of friendship!

Dr. Ali Syed, our serendipitous meeting and Lab-Line connection has been a glorious gift to my life and my book.

James Knowles, Sarah Coombs, and Arlene Lynes, your book seller's experience, knowledge, time, and advice have been invaluable.

Lynne Carreiro, thank you for helping me recognize that my father was the avant-garde CCO (Chief Compliance Officer) of Lab-Line.

Nancy Karasak, as a voracious reader, I knew you would be an extraordinary peer reader. I appreciated the time you took to read my manuscript and offer me your candid opinion.

Debby Kuzniar, Chenoa Lorenzo, Erin Murphy, Shelby Steffens, and Tricia Wallace, your mindful yoga classes at Silver Lotus Yoga Studio have helped to keep my body and mind healthy, creative, and flexible.

TJ Butler, Jad N. Lahoud, Jill Winalis Looff, Nedd Neddersen, Matthew Primack, and Marsha L. Turner, I appreciate kindhearted testimonials and praise for *No Bunk*.

Caryn Amster (Bubelah), I appreciated your professional story, testimonial contribution, and peer readership, which added value and encouragement to my writing process.

Laurie Buchanan, I valued your rapid and excited "from the get go" response as a peer reader, your extensive and detailed comments, and authentic and meaningful testimonial as a "savvy" fellow author.

Courtney Childers, I am grateful for your excitement about *No Bunk*, from the first time we spoke, your time to be a peer reader, and your enthusiastic testimonial.

Jeff Lewis, I appreciate your personal and professional comments as a peer reader. I loved, *"I would have enjoyed meeting and talking to your father because he was someone I could relate to and you felt like you knew him."* I know he also would have enjoyed talking with you.

Lauren Biddle Plummer, I needed your editing skills and suggestions to breathe life into my ideas and keep my creativity focused.

Chris Geimer, I am delighted with the *No Bunk, Just BS* cover you designed for my book. I also appreciated your skills to format the photos and visuals that I needed for the book.

John Bond (JB), your always dependable and generous professional expertise, truthfulness, advice (reminiscences), and friendship contributed to making my *No Bunk* dream a reality.

"Cousin" Marilyn Elrod, I am eternally grateful for you and your attention to detail, helpful suggestions, and the time you took to carefully and lovingly read my manuscript about your Aunt Sylvia and Uncle Al.

Raymond J. Kayal, Jr. I knew you were the perfect person to write the Foreword for *No Bunk*. I am honored and humbled by your authentic, personal, and beautiful words. I am blessed by our friendship and our loving "Florida Family."

Joshua, Noah, Sheryl, Kelly, Ashton, Yasmin, Jonah, Michelle, and John, I am most grateful that you are loving and joyful blessings in our family! ILYMTTCT.

Joshua Glazov, all the time you took to write your detailed review and meticulous notes about the manuscript and loving comments about your grandparents were superb contributions to my revision processes and are profoundly appreciated!

Jordan Glazov (Jordy), our life partnership, your everlasting love, our trip to Lab-Line to retrieve my father's books and memorabilia, your precise editing, patience, and enthusiastic encouragement to write *No Bunk* are treasures I appreciate and cherish! AMLFE&E

About the Author

Sheila Newman Glazov is a best-selling author, award-winning professional speaker, internationally known personality expert, and passionate educator.

Sheila has appeared on CNN, NBC, ABC, FOX, LIFETIME and WGN TV. She has been interviewed on internet programs and radio stations throughout the United States and in Brazil, and featured in the Wall Street Journal, Chicago Tribune, Chicago Sun Times, Daily Herald and PRAVDA newspapers, iG (largest Brazilian internet portal), Happy Women (Portuguese magazine), Selling Power, HR, Women's World, Chicago Parent, Seventeen, and Enterprising Women magazines, and the Discover Card and Quill Corporation national customer newsletters. Today's Chicago Woman newspaper selected Sheila as one of "100 Women Making a Difference."

Her innovative style has won Sheila praise for her programs and workshops in conference rooms and classrooms in the United States and around the world. Encouraging adults and children to recognize and respect the best in themselves and others is the essence of her programs and books. Sheila helps people improve their job performance, communicate more effectively, resolve conflicts quickly, build healthier and more harmonious relationships, and learn life-long skills that are like multiplication tables, that people never forget!

Sheila earned her Bachelor of Science degree in education from the Ohio State University. She is a certified Authorized Entity Trainer for the State of Illinois and a Registry Approved Trainer for the State of Illinois Gateways to Opportunity Registry.

Sheila has taught third grade, high school ESL, and has been an adjunct faculty member of William Rainey Harper College and a guest instructor at DePaul, Penn State, and Northwood Universities. Sheila has also written curricula for the Colorado School of Medicine.

Sheila lives in the Chicagoland area with her husband and family.

For more information about Sheila, her books, programs, musical theater productions, and her support for JDRF, visit her website: **www.sheilaglazov.com**.

Author's Professional Development Programs

Sheila makes the art of understanding yourself and others fascinating and fun. Program attendees immediately benefit from Sheila's innovative and participatory programs, which are always interactive and engaging, never tedious or tiresome. Sheila personalizes every program to satisfy each client's unique culture, environment, meeting, or conference.

The content of Sheila's programs is relevant, achieves constructive, long-term outcomes, and promotes enthusiastic participation. Participants quickly transfer and apply their new knowledge to their workplace. Sheila can also adapt her programs to provide attendees with Continuing Education Units (CEU).

For more information about Sheila's educational, entertaining, and engaging **No Bunk, Just BS (Business Sense)** and **What Color Is Your Brain?® Programs** for your business conferences and meetings, professional development events, association conventions contact Sheila at **847.526.9039** or **sheila@sheilaglazov.com** and visit her website **www.sheilaglazov.com**.

Author's Other Books

What Color Is Your Brain?® A Fun and Fascinating Approach to Understanding Yourself and Others is a quick and easy personality profile that helps adults and children quickly understand the differences in their personalities. *What Color Is Your Brain?*® has been translated into Portuguese and traditional Chinese.

What Color Is Your Brain?® When Caring for Patients helps Health Care Professionals discover their unique Brain Colors, decode their patients' and co-workers' personalities, understand why their co-workers and patients see them way they do, and how the different Brain Color perspective influence workplace relationships!

Princess Shayna's Invisible Visible Gift is an exquisitely illustrated and engaging children's chapter book adaptation of Sheila's book, *What Color Is Your Brain?*®. *Princess Shayna's Invisible Visible Gift* and has been adapted into musical theater productions.

The *Teacher's Activity Guide for "Princess Shayna's Invisible Visible Gift"* is a teacher's resource to apply *Princess Shayna's* valuable lessons in the classrooms.

Sheila allocates 10% of the royalties from the sale of the books listed above to the **JDRF** (Juvenile Diabetes Research Foundation).

Purr-fect Pals: A Kid, A Cat and Diabetes is a picture/activity/resource book designed to offer comfort, education, and encouragement to children and their families who live with the challenges of Type 1 Diabetes (T1D) and Type 2 Diabetes (T2D).

Sheila allocates100% of the royalties from the sale of ***Purr-fect Pals: A Kid, A Cat and Diabetes*** to **JDRF** (Juvenile Diabetes Research Foundation).

www.ingramcontent.com/pod-product-compliance
Lightning Source LLC
Chambersburg PA
CBHW070729220326
41598CB00024BA/3364